MAKE YOUR MARK: PERSONAL BRANDING THROUGH "ON-PURPOSE" LIVING

MAKE YOUR MARK: PERSONAL BRANDING THROUGH "ON-PURPOSE" LIVING

The Dream Big, Brand Smart Guide to Blazing a Trail In Your Life

Courtney R. Rhodes

ISBN-13: 9780692833919
ISBN-10: 0692833919

Acknowledgments

I want to thank my husband, Leslie Bond, Jr. and daughter, Jala Clarke Wilson for pushing and supporting me daily to get Make Your Mark: Personal Branding through "On-Purpose" Living out of my mind and onto the pages of this guide. Your love for and confidence in me gives me the courage to "do my work," you make me better, stronger, and happier. I wish to thank Nicole Mitchell and Levolia Rhodes (Mom); you're my earth angels. To my siblings, Byron, Alicia, and Ryan, thanks for a lifetime of laughs and believing in me. To Nathaniel Rhodes (Nay), my father and heavenly angel, thank you for making me forever a daddy's girl. I'm beyond bless God gave me just the tribe I needed.

To Steve Ewing, my longest-standing client and friend, thank you for the years of opportunity to work with your dynamic personal brand, Wade Ford, Motor Trend, and Ford Motor Company. I'm grateful to the sponsors, vendors, and partners you've introduced me to and allowed me to work with over the last seven years. Your commitment to profitability, community development, and philanthropy inspires me. Debra Cartwright, thank you for entrusting me to license the use of your beautiful illustrations in bringing life to Make Your Mark: Personal Branding Through "On-Purpose" Living. © Debra Cartwright 2017

I thank the Public Relations Society of America's Regional Conference at Georgia Southern for opening my eyes to the enormous pride and eagerness college students and millennials take in leveraging their own value, voices, and goals. Your eagerness to become both successful and fulfilled in your own lives lit a fire in my soul. Your energy and zest to make a difference in the world reinvigorated me on my own path. You gave me tremendous inspiration. I'm beyond grateful for the positive energy and gratitude you showed me during your 2015 regional conference, BrandMe. Your gracious e-mails, notes, and tweets fueled something in me. They sent me into a sort of midlife crisis that shook up my own psyche and forced me to take an intimate look at my life, my values, and the people I'm committed to serving. Your inquisitiveness moved me to share as much insight, guidance, and thought-leadership in personal development and personal branding as I have to share.

Introduction

Are you gearing up to launch a new business or blog? Are you ready to grow your visibility as the personality behind an established business or blog? Maybe you're a recent graduate looking to establish yourself in your industry; or you want to get up to speed on the topic of personal branding to build awareness around your unique competences. Your branding initiative should take the things you love and support unwaveringly and allow them to direct the path for your life's journey. Use this book as a guide that'll keep the disciplines of self-discovery and branding at the forefront of your life.

I know too many people who've postponed their dreams, placing them on the back burner to how their lives have unfolded. They're forced to spend the majority of their time working in jobs that aren't meaningful or fulfilling. Some have chosen to believe "that's just the way life is." I happen to strongly disagree. While I understand doing what needs to be done to support your basic needs; still, many of those people tend to circle back to their dreams once those basic needs are met. The sooner you commit to supporting both your short-term and long-term goals the earlier you'll enjoy the benefits of becoming your ideal self and exploring your fullest potential.

The content in this book represents my unique perspective as it emerge from my education, professional career, and life lessons along with countless interactions with authentic, fulfilled, and empowered individuals. I've created the *Make Your Mark* series to share the firsthand experience, knowledge, and awareness I've gained spending nearly twenty years working to promote, market, and align myself with socially conscious and impactful brands throughout the country. Whether I was working in the development department at Gilman School in Baltimore, Maryland; the reservations department at Caves Valley Golf Club in Owings Mills, Maryland; or the president's office at the NAACP's national office in Baltimore, Maryland, I was blessed to spend the early part of my career working for and learning from brands driven by strong social and community-advancement missions. Those experiences solidified the foundation for the work I would find soul in.

I'm a supporter of The Gallup Organization, a research-based, glob al performance-management consulting company, Clifton Strengths Finder system. Gallup's strengths solutions encourage people to lead with their strengths as a means to be more engaged, productive, and fulfilled. Gallup created the science of strengths from over fifty years of research and offers a myriad of leadership tools from the Clifton StrengthsFinder assessment, to strengths coaching kits, and best-selling books. According to Gallup's Strengths Center, people who are allowed to use their strengths daily are six times more likely to be engaged on the job, while teams that focus on their strengths are 12.5 percent more productive. Throughout my management career at one of America's largest media companies, I was coached to lead with my strengths, and I managed my team by theirs. To this day, it's been that leadership philosophy and guidance I've valued the most in my career. My top five strengths are strategic, futuristic, relator, self-assurance, and maximizer in that order. I've come to accept as natural as it feels for many of us to want to spend our time working on improving our weaknesses; our confidence and best self lives in refining, mastering, and leading with our strengths.

Throughout my career, I've recognized interesting commonalities. The most prevalent being people's deeply rooted desire to flirt with depth to find meaning: self-actualization, fulfillment, and significant connections. Recently it became blaringly apparent to me that today's emotionally charged, politically divided, and often chaotic social climate birthed a surge of people who crave more meaning in their everyday existences and influence over their own destinies.

Inspired by the drive to make their positive mark in the world, people want their voices heard, talents shared, stories told, and communities supported. We're yearning to live in ways that nurture and feed our own deeply rooted desires. We're committed to supporting and serving things that matter to us, drive our motivation, and expose our purpose. Turmoil and unrest drive our innate instincts, thereby nudging our desire to connect, communicate, and collaborate in like-minded communities to make a certain impact. Certainly this mind-set has led Americans to retool their businesses or career paths in ways that purposely serve their realities—the people, communities, and causes significant to them.

The four pillars of personal branding success I share are proven, strategic, and tactical best practices from corporate branding, marketing communications, and advertising principles. My intention is to ensure this book guides you through extracting what's authentic, purposeful, and brilliant about you. Then assist you in packaging and positioning that story with your mission, vision, and goals. You'll discover the personal attributes to best lead your brand and explore ways to maximize your brand's components to realize your fullest potential. Whether you want to explore new career opportunities, launch or rebrand a business or blog, snag more clients, or enjoy the gratification of being more purposeful in your life, this guide is here to help you. Within this book, you'll find an accountability partner to show and remind you that you can do it!

I've developed my stance working in various brand-marketing, advertising, and media-sales roles throughout my career. I've assisted numerous businesses and people in finding clarity around what's unique and different about what they have to offer. Together, we have subsequently packaged and positioned people, products, and services. After graduating from Morgan State University in 1998 with a bachelor of arts in communications, I completed a Small Business Administration (SBA) Women Entrepreneurship of Baltimore certification program. In 2001, I earned a master of arts in publications design from the University of Baltimore. My postgraduate career includes cool opportunities in advertising sales and brand marketing with top media companies like iHeartMedia (formerly Clear Channel), Meredith Corporation (a CBS television station), and *Uptown Magazine*. As an employee and consultant, I've worked with cutting-edge brands, extremely talented clients, and mentors who helped me realize my own potential.

Your creative soul is guided by its own energy, curiosity, and possibilities. This sacred seed of authenticity is fueled by its need to connect and make a distinct mark in a world of endless possibilities. It represents your differences in ideas and priorities, like a logo or tagline. It's both a representation of and the driving force behind your core truths—the ones you feel in your heart and envision in your mind, whether or not you choose to nurture it. Sadly, the seed of that authentic mark is sometimes bound and never fully realized because of its carrier's own fears, limited beliefs, and distractions.

What does this mean for you? Nurture, develop, and communicate your potential. Use this guide along with your personal branding journal in the back to help you filter through the cluttered world of branding so you can make good, meaningful, and lasting impressions in your life. Become known for what you represent and the value you offer to the world. Be authentic, build trust, help others, and do stellar work over and over again. I hate to disappoint you, but it's just that simple.

Reflecting on my own life's journey, I realize that I did not understand this early on. Yet I've been branding myself most of my life. As a young girl, when not exploring the interesting outdoor adventures of Chicken Creek Road, I loved participating in beauty pageants and modeling in local television commercials and newspaper spreads. I developed an interest for training for both, and that passion fueled the foundation upon which I've built my career and brand. I captured my first title as Tiny Miss Bonner Elementary as a toothless kindergartener, and throughout my primary and secondary school career, I won my fair share of beauty pageant titles. In middle and high school, I repurposed my grandparents' car shed as a pageant stage to provide training to other girls in my community. Although I didn't charge for my services and money was never my motivation, I appreciated the tips I collected doing it. I took my obligation seriously, having tremendous pride in what

I taught my contestants. More times than not, my girls brought home the crown. Until my college days, etiquette and modeling classes were the courses I found myself naturally engaged in. Those primary years of running free and uninhibited exploration of the world around me built the foundation for the things I would eventually pursue, the people with whom I would connect, and the ideals around which my life would soon revolve.

While in college, I completed a work study at Morgan State University's development office. I interned for the fashion office at Nordstrom, Girl's Life magazine, and 92Q radio station in Baltimore. Why? I recognized my passions and I was curious to explore as many career options as possible supporting them. My internships and work opportunities led me to further develop an appreciation for the power of communications to shape perceptions, garner influence, and drive sales. Those experiences later influenced me to pursue my graduate work in publications design: to study the integration of words, images, and design to translate ideas into print and other media. Meanwhile, during graduate school, I participated in another work study under Karen Lee, who was director of scouting at Elite Models in New York City: a top modeling agency whose models were at the forefront of shaping perceptions, garnering influence, and driving sales for some of America's top retail brands.

Those college experiences reflected my own passion for personal development and exploring one's own wiring. I believe we're all born with a sacred seed planted in our hearts, wrapped within our unique DNA, representing the divine mark that our lives individually have the potential to realize. Each seed is as different as the journeys they inspire.

The blessings of financial freedom and career success (which are always relative) are remarkable; however, I'm driven by my own dreams—and there is nothing more rewarding than sharing my knowledge in the world by serving the people and causes I care about. On most journeys, there are peaks, valleys, and deep curves. Every now and again, we've all endured those uncomfortably bumpy roads with toe-curling caution lights at every turn. That's the beauty of experiencing every facet of your travels. Nonetheless and no matter what, in order to get to your destination, you *must* keep moving forward; sometimes at a turtle's pace, other times a Tesla's. We all need to develop the insight to accept when it's time to take a break to refuel, regroup, or just reflect. Conversely, in identifying the goals for your brand and pinpointing the gifts you have to provide in the world, you must commit to live, sleep, and breathe them. Any other possibility is a copout, robbing yourself of the opportunity to grant your own potential a winner's try. You know the saying, right? "Winners never quit, and quitters never win." That couldn't be any more significant when considering your own efforts in pursuit of the goals and aspirations you hold for your life. Remember, success—like balance—is a flexible word. "Success" for you will look different from "success" for your parents, friends, and associates. Why? Because we're all wired differently. Your own sacred seed—your DNA, core values, capabilities, personality attributes, and passion—have blessed you with a unique perspective, preferences, mission, and journey through self-realization.

Your life is your story to experience, message, and share as you choose. Recognizing your dreams is your duty and your obligation to fulfill with your greatest potential. Personal branding through "on-purpose" living, when executed properly, is an ideal platform to lead you there.

Why Branding Matters

You can only become truly accomplished at something you love. Don't make money your goal. Instead pursue the things you love doing, and then do them so well that people can't take their eyes off you.

—Dr. Maya Angelou

The word *brand* means to burn, originating from thousands of years of branding to denote ownership or origin. Brands were applied to cattle and human slaves for over four thousand years. During the period of transatlantic enslavement, millions of slaves were branded with metal branding irons, marking their owners' initials. Simultaneously, during the seventeenth century in Europe and France, branding was used to punish and identify fugitives; in India, it was used for religious denotations.

With its colorful history, body branding is still used by people all around the globe to decorate their physiques with tribal and organizational affiliation. Corporate branding is documented as starting toward the end of the nineteenth century, concurrent with the Industrial Revolution.

The establishment of department stores advanced the way people shopped. As the era introduced wider ranges of products available on the market, competition was introduced among the suppliers. As a means to differentiate products and create consumer loyalty branding was employed to communicate unique differences. As manufacturing technology advanced and distribution channels matured, companies were able to mass produce consumer products and achieve broader penetration. Companies also began to identify their customer base and thus refine and target their product messaging.

Mass marketing introduced consumers to the concept of shopping for leisure in their spare time; and people started to identify the products they purchased with their lifestyle and status. Proctor and Gamble, one of America's largest marketing machines, was established in 1837 as a soap and candlemaker. The company utilized branding as a discipline to distinguish the various products they offered, in order to gain market share in a market where twelve other candlemakers already existed.

Leading up to the 1950's, fueled by an economic boom, the evolution of manufacturers applying specialized marketing strategies for each of its brands, and the beginning of television advertising: brands became popular household names. By the end of 1960's the majority of manufactures of consumer packaged goods were hiring marketing professionals and assigning a dedicated brand manager to control the strategy behind their individual brands. By the mid 1980's, driven by affluence, the evolution in mass communication, and accessible transportation a large expansion of global advertising agencies popped up with offices in major cities throughout the world. By the middle part of the 1990's branding was abundant. The discipline entered into categories in which hadn't been traditional branding sectors. By the late 90's American's witnessed the emergence of the dot-com era and the unfortunate propaganda of over branding; as the value of many technology companies became exaggerated with promises they couldn't deliver on.

Fast-forward to today: thousands of iconic American brands have remained relevant for decades through their ability to separate themselves from the competition and build value with their target consumers. Today brands play a prominent role in the lives of millions of Americans, while branding has moved beyond just marketing and advertising professionals. Branding has evolved into a discipline that has become a requirement in most industries, merely to stand out and survive. According to

Psychology Today, Americans are subjected to between three thousand and ten thousand different brand exposures on a daily basis.

A brand is the promise of something. That variable being intangible, it could represent a promise of quality, a sense of prestige, heritage, lifestyle, or a proven result. Brands offer differentiating factors, making it easy for the marketplace to choose between the many competing products, services, or people vying for the same opportunity.

From my viewpoint, personal branding is the discipline of using corporate-branding techniques to identify the distinct offerings of a person and then educating other people about those ideals, capabilities, character, and overarching story of that person. The primary function being branding's ability to transform a complex human being with a distinct yet multifaceted story of who they are and what they stand for using simple and clear communications.

Your brand is composed of many elements: your name, character, reputation, skill set, image, attributes, and a persona that differentiates you from others. Although it can't be touched, it represents a degree of apparent value, making it the largest variable in your personal success. It embodies the mental picture and feeling others have when they think of you. It's the vibe, reputation, and observations people have about you as an individual. It represents the sum of the occurrences, competency, and personal energy you exude when other people are interacting directly with you or messages they've processed about you. In today's marketplace, you're a walking, talking, breathing billboard. Everything you say, do, and support as well as the demeanor with which you communicate it, shapes how people identify with you.

Your brand is never how you think about or perceive yourself, it is *only* in how others perceive you—and that isn't necessarily always a fair or a true depiction of the wholeness of you. Still, it's what your associates, colleagues, classmates, professors, family, clients, audience, potential clients, or vendors have to say about you when you're not in the room. That's why it's important to remain authentic but self-aware as you consciously shape the brand you desire into one you'll feel proud about. People want to work and associate themselves with brands they like, trust, and feel are competent. As a result, you have to resonate with your target market. The more you connect with them through positive touch points, the more likely they'll buy into the product, service, or value you offer. This guide gives you strategies on how to hone and direct your brand, but your consistent behavior over time is what will ultimately translate into what your brand will become.

Personal branding was not a part of my career conversations in the '90s. However, passion, interests, personal development, strengths, reputation, character, and business acumen were, and your personal brand is simply a beautiful combination of them all. It may appear like the concept was born overnight, but that couldn't be any further from the truth. We just weren't Googling everything and stalking each other via social media in earlier times. Still, when people inquired about someone, the question was often asked, "What's their story?" Your brand was, and will be, your reputation merged with observations of your interests and passions, social and professional associations, connections, and behaviors.

Strategic components of brand marketing, the Internet, and social media platforms- present a golden opportunity for you to share your voice and build your brand. They offer you unlimited chances to extend yourself to access robust online communities. Consider yourself a free agent. While for some, it appears unfairly simple to capture the hearts and minds of an all-too-aspirational audience and grow an empire. For others, it seems daunting and too exhausting to maneuver online communities. Equipped with the best practices culled from corporate branding, marketing communications, and advertising principles it's easier than ever to build your consistent in- person and online persona. In the very nature of putting yourself on blast for the world to know, you'll be motivated to put forth your best efforts, challenge your comfort zone, and follow your own Yellow Brick Road.

The Internet represents a chance for you that never existed before in history: the power of accessibility that can reach thousands of people for little to no cost. What the tool is not is a forgiving option for people with an identifiable disconnection between the stories they share online versus the daily behaviors they engage in. Don't make this mistake because you can't erase it. Take ownership of your digital presence or it will take control of you. Consider the relentless feminist whose brand story includes working toward women's rights and equality. Contemplate how your perception of her might change as you witness her verbally attack another woman she doesn't perceive as favorably using her voice. That depicts branding gone wrong. We're all guilty of it from time to time; whether online or in- person, we've said something that doesn't depict the larger part of who we are. You know what I'm talking about: the "you" you've the potential to become versus the "you" who haphazardly allows your emotions to let life unravel on social media as it may. The very discipline of branding requires you to be all in, as much as humanly possible, having your behaviors on- and offline wholeheartedly support, communicate, and exemplify what you believe.

If you enjoy helping and working with women and own a tax service specializing in servicing the needs of women entrepreneurs, they're your target market. Thus, you should work passionately and diligently to service their needs and provide them with cutting-edge service. As a means to further connect with this group, you could volunteer with innovative business-development programs for women, host tax and financial-planning workshops, or speak on panels to share your insight. Not only will you get a paycheck, attract more clients, and achieve your own brand goals through your extended service, but you'll also be building your career around your values, capabilities, and passions.

The overarching part of your brand-building success is the process of establishing both value and trust with others. We're all people, vulnerably human, perfectly flawed through our uniquely mortal existence. Variety and difference are at the center of your power—your sacred seed of authenticity, dreams, and original ideas. No matter what or how similar they may taste, you'll never see Coca-Cola wrap a Coke label around a bottle of Pepsi, or a Starbucks sign outside of your local Dunkin' Donuts. Instead, branding takes the essence of what you are, while allowing you to explore new possibilities. It permits you to discover and embrace your own brand potential through bringing your special talents, gifts, and capabilities to the forefront of what you do.

In a multitude of industries, traditional ways of doing things aren't working anymore—and finding the balance between traditional industry standards and relevancy to profitability or the bottom line is often complicated. Define and embrace your authenticity while finding your comfortable place in an ever-evolving culture of what is acceptable and what's not. What feels right for you? What doesn't? Understand history and know the rules of the masses; from there, design your own set of operating standards to serve as your personal, nonnegotiable guide for living. Play by someone else's rules, and you'll win or lose by someone else's standards. Play by your own, and you're destined to win or lose by your own account. To succeed in "on-purpose" living, accept that you must absolutely experience life with gusto, meaning, and a sense of self-expression that validates: I'm being seen, I'm being heard, and my life matters. You were created to make your distinct mark on the world by contributing your special gifts and making a positive impact in life. That mark is none other than the unique will of your heart, working in tandem with the vision in your mind.

As you embrace playing by your own rules, you should employ your own inner guidance system, pursue your own desires, be good to people, and do cool things. Consider doing stuff you identify as important, relevant, and ideal for you to develop the confidence you need for what's next in your life. Surrender to personal branding as your partner through self-realization, accepting that it'll push you to new levels of discomfort. For every milestone of growth, you'll be required to master unknown things, so embrace the new experiences along with the challenges they'll present.

At every new height, the vibrancy of your mark will direct the next phase of discovery, and the process repeats itself. No doubt, you'll have pit stops. At times, you'll feel like you're moving backward—and you very well may be, but that's okay. I've been there; we've all been there, but ironically, it's oftentimes in the frustration of those valleys where clarity emerges, courage is found, and we surrender to those subtle whispers. It's all a part of learning the necessary skills, lessons, and fortitude to thrust you forward. Remember, the seed of your mark knows what's possible and has no boundaries or timetable. If you're not taking charge of your life, you could easily fall into the misfortune of always being a chaser, chasing something on the outside, something not real—or worse, someone else's dream.

YOU HAVE A PERSONAL BRAND, WHETHER YOU DIRECT IT OR NOT

In today's marketplace, if you're generic, you're expendable. Conversely, by building value and cultivating rock-solid proficiencies around something your market wants or needs, you can create a demand for yourself. Be unique and try to position yourself in front of trends. Research the direction your space, industry, or business is headed in. Pay attention to the needs of that trajectory and correlating technologies that align those needs with what your brand offers. Consider those discoveries as potential sweet spots or a niche you can provide. I'm not suggesting a growing niche is always possible or simple to identify; nonetheless, if you can do it, it's a sure way to align yourself along a path to uniqueness.

Organizations invest in employees, clients, or partners they're most comfortable working with. They selectively choose to employ, cultivate, and promote personal brands that align best with their own corporate culture or the vision they have for it. Of course, for corporate America, it's both natural and safe to implement successfully proven best practices to emulate what "traditionally works" for their hiring practice. If it isn't broken, why fix it? There is enormous value in diversity, and while diversity is a fairly recent concept in America, at minimum it requires people with hiring authority and employment input to acknowledge their own bias and explore outside their own comfort zones of familiar territory. Why is this important to know? Because there'll be organizations where you just won't be a good fit, and the sooner you can identify that and move on (or better yet, avoid the opportunity all together), the better it will be for your own sanity, confidence, and progression. Don't get it twisted; there is always an opportunity to grow and learn in any experience. However, with a clear vision of where you're headed and the ideals you're committed to, a detour against that plan is never going to be the most efficient or fruitful route.

If you're wondering why bother with personal branding anyway, let me say this: to brand or not to brand is a valid question, one that's certainly conversation-worthy. John McLaughlin, one of my favorite graduate-school professors at the University of Baltimore's School of Communications Design, believed that for corporate brands, effective branding is the most treasured sustainability key for winning long-term growth and success. In the same spirit, personal branding gives you the ability to cast a clear vision of what you stand for, without running the risk of becoming a blur of an option, just another candidate, or in the worst-case scenario, one whose potential was never fully developed or recognized.

Consider the spoken and unspoken culture, rules, and standards of the industries and organizations you're seeking to work for or collaborate with. Know your own boundaries, and choose to err on the side of conservatism if something feels too risky within your own brand communications. You should be authentic, but the degree of creativity in the communication and messaging of your brand's identification, persona, voice, and associations should align with the acceptable standards of your industry. Certainly, there may be times you have to compromise your own creative expression for the bigger picture of achieving your goals.

In our connected world, people who are willing to commit to their dreams and work their plans are pushing new boundaries and creating the lives they've envisioned for themselves. So why does branding matter? Because authentically making your mark is a quite layered but worthwhile process that can serve as your accountability partner along your journey through realizing your fullest potential.

You are not and will never be a brand. You *have* a brand, and that brand has a story: a visual, verbal, and energetic essence that is flexible and forever evolving. You have genuine experiences, ideals, mission, dreams, and a reputation you'll continue to mold and shape. Collectively, they will set the tone for the expectations others will place upon you. It's an implied value between you and them that makes them believe that when they see or interact with you, they will receive a certain quality of service, expertise, and care—or lack thereof. With clarity around your goals for your life, you can determine which of your capabilities can best lead you to attract "on-purpose" opportunities that will best inspire you to spark your brilliance and accomplish those dreams.

On purpose, structure your brand around the things that are most important to you and the people and causes you want to help. I'm not saying making an impactful mark and shaping your authentically "on-purpose" brand is simple; it isn't. But the good news is that following this guide is easy. Not everyone is disciplined enough to do the work. If you're ready to accomplish more in your life, are willing to explore your own wiring, and are determined to put in the work, you can direct a brand and realize goals for yourself that'll make you proud. I believe you can do this, and there's no better time to begin than now. The world needs you, your brilliance, and the uniquely individual sacred mark only you can offer.

2

How Personal Branding Works

No one is perfect: we weren't meant to be. We're meant to unravel, discover, and honor our own highest goodness.

—Courtney R. Rhodes

Following a cohesive branding model is a proven strategy to keep your communication messages focused toward the people, places, and causes that matter most to you. It gives you the control to consciously direct the impressions you make in the minds of others; shaping the perception they'll form of you.

Your personal brand's reputation is being established by a trust-based currency. The essence of it has to exude authenticity, competency, and trust. Who you portray online should perfectly mirror who you are offline, or you'll lose trust and fall short in establishing your brand's value. If you're an advocate for animal rights and you work at a chicken farm slaughtering chickens, you'll be hard pressed to find fulfillment or brand alignment. Sure, it may very well pay the bills, but it'll serve as a soul killer in the meantime.

The people you interact with already have a perception of you, if it's only the "short, opinionated, brown-skinned girl from Goose Creek with the inverted bob who went to the College of Charleston." Everything you do wields influence over how others view you, including the way you groom yourself, how you behave at social gatherings, communicate online, and treat the guy who changes your oil.

Ask yourself, "Who is the 'me' others know?" People who know you have interacted with your character, but what about those who haven't connected with or met you? They don't know you, yet some will naturally form an opinion about you based on your social media profiles and online activities. If you haphazardly share random information about yourself or rely on others to educate those folks about you, they may process a sense of "you" represented by only a small snippet of what you've embodied. Inadvertently, you may put forth a brand that is inadequately composed of bits and pieces of random accumulated impressions you've mindlessly orchestrated.

Unless you've been hiding under a rock, without social media handles, network affiliations, or causes that you've embraced, you have a brand. The moment someone hears your name, their mind pulls up imprints of memories that previously molded their beliefs about you. Their philosophies may originate from the result of working directly with you, an organization you're affiliated with, a web search on your name, good or bad publicity they've heard or seen, word of mouth, your social media presence, and other mentions or images that embedded thoughts about you in their minds.

Some people's memories house a myriad of perceptions about you, while others will only have faint (if any) impressions at all. Regardless of whether the beliefs others hold about you are vast or few, good or bad, accurate or inaccurate, it shapes their interpretation of your brand. Those imprints influence how those people interact with or react to you. The more you understand your brand, the better suited you are to guide your own behaviors and the actions directly impacting it. A brand that aligns with what you want to convey about yourself and achieve in your life will always be your best offense.

Personal branding works because it's both the foundation that allows you to communicate distinguishing points of value and what makes you different from the competition. It defines the vehicle that guides you to deliver on your unique promise of value over and over again. That brand promise and the value it provides become the commitment of your brand to the people you'll serve. How well you deliver on your brand promise, coupled with everything you do over time, builds trust and competency—or contradiction for your one-of-a kind promise. So personal branding only works successfully when you do. Therefore, it's critical to choose a promise that feels second nature for you: exemplifying your commitment to the people you've identified you want to serve, while supporting the mission, goals, and dreams you've identified for your life.

In guiding and educating others about your brand, your goal is to live up to your brand's promise every time people connect with you. Keep in mind it doesn't matter whether the connection you're making is in person, through your personal website, newsletter, social media, a web search, advertising, word of mouth, or other forms of communication. It's all shaping your brand. Every single encounter influences the perceptions forming your brand, fortifying or defying the brand promise you've made.

Branding requires you to intentionally communicate messages and provide experiences that influence what people believe, or more precisely, what your brand inspires them to think. Throughout the branding process, there are numerous psychological influences at play, each firing at the highest emotional and intellectual levels of our brains. We're wired to make assessments based on a combination of emotional factors that steer our attention and influence our thinking. These aspects include things like brand identification, brand affiliations, the receiver's own internal state, and their social contexts around the impressions they process. We weigh the impressions we receive about others against our own value systems, beliefs, needs, preferences, and religious and social biases. Never assume that because you send clear messages to others, they're certain to be translated in the way you'd hoped for. Nevertheless, as you interact on- and offline with others, signals are sent to the brains of those you're communicating with. Ultimately, how those signals trigger a response in their brains form their position on your brand.

Strong and positive resonance, emotional connectivity, and familiarity translate into your brand being viewed favorably, whereas those who are perceived with negative associations, no emotional connectivity, or dissonance could spark little to nothing or a negative assessment. For that reason, I can't reiterate enough that how you choose to show up in your life is 100 percent your responsibility; meanwhile, how others process that is never your charge. Although personal branding works by providing a stage from which you're liberated to distinguish who you are, what you offer, and what you stand for in a marketplace among clutter and competition. What it can't do is make you the flavor of preference or likeable to everyone. No matter what, you can't control how another individual will process the information they've been exposed to. You don't have the luxury of controlling others, so you should by no means allow that to deter you from your own authenticity, mission, and goals. There is tremendous power in uniqueness and diversity; accordingly, there's a market or audience for everyone. In identifying and shaping the messages you want to communicate with others, you'll establish yourself in ways that position you and the value you bring to the table, making you recognizably more visible to the people you've set out to target.

This leads me to emphasize that having five thousand random social media followers means very little if they aren't like-minded individuals in your target demographic or are engaged with the things you share online. It's difficult to quantify engagement, but a brand with five hundred social media followers and fifty likes (or a 10 percent engagement), has garnered more influence and a higher engagement rate than the brand with five thousand followers and fifty likes (a 1 percent engagement). The advantage is your ability to tailor your specific brand's story, messages, and content in ways that emotionally connect your story with the market you're serving.

You have a reputation, an image, a persona, and most likely, you engage on at least one social platform. Think about your favorite celebrities or public figures. What makes them your favorite? Is it the information they share on social media, the causes they support, how they resonate with you when they speak, their talents, their personal style, or a combination of it all? No matter who comes to mind, the impressions they send have successfully made a favorable and significant impact on your mind about who they are and what they represent.

It's irrelevant if you're a publicist, sales professional, doctor, financial analyst, blogger, lawyer, teacher, or entrepreneur; you'll benefit from cultivating your personal brand in ways that leverage your proficiencies, increase exposure, expand your networks, and solidify opportunities. There are people listening to what you're saying, watching your moves, and following your social media activity. They're actively processing what you've shared, and forming opinions about you at every touch point they encounter. That's how branding works, and the discipline will continue to differentiate people, places, and things as long as the human mind continues to process information the way it has for thousands of years.

Assuredly, your mother knows you're the smartest, most strategic, go-getting, strikingly charming, brown-eyed girl east of the Mississippi. What about the human resources director or hiring manager at the Fortune 500 company you've been dreaming of working for, or the client whose business you would love to earn? What do they know about you? As you identify the unique value you offer, package those proficiencies, and message that story to everyone who will listen your personal brand will flourish.

3

Define Your Authenticity: Embrace Who You Are

Be yourself; everyone else is already taken.

—*Oscar Wilde*

Authenticity is about finding clarity and having conviction around who you are. In 1989, when I was fourteen years old, my grandfather, who was eighty, and the most authentic character I've known, died of complications from arterial sclerosis. He and my grandmother had a robust influence on my upbringing. Early on, 'Daddy' taught me "in order to earn respect, you treat people well, have compassion, and give service." He encouraged me and all of his grandchildren to learn as much as we could, work harder than the next person, do our jobs well, and never let anyone tell us what we can't do. With that kind of guidance, I knew I could choose my own path. His words were always wise, and he lived life accordingly, as one of the few people I've known to always say what he meant and mean what he said. Daddy's brand was one of a devoted family man, a respectable minister, and proud Democrat. He may not have supported Democrats' views on every issue, but that was irrelevant. For him, Democrats were for the people. There was no gray area; it was his conviction, and Daddy was a man of conviction.

Understanding who you are and embracing that sacred seed of authenticity is the foundation of your brand. While the most important function of embracing your seed of authenticity is welcoming the space to discover, grow, and support your highest existence. Without that clarity you risk marketing something that doesn't represent you. In this chapter you'll define your core values, capabilities, personal brand attributes, and passion. Throughout the branding process you'll defer to those qualities to hold yourself accountable to support behaviors leading your towards your mission and goals; and crafting a brand story that'll position your brand the way you'd like to be viewed. Use your personal branding journal in the back to make notes and complete the branding exercises.

Being authentic requires you to commit your life to the uniqueness of its individualized path. Never become hostage to behaviors that don't support your purpose. Living purposely is the priority for your life. Having said this, the decision to brand should always be secondary to and in support of your ever-evolving identity.

Making your mark is twofold. First, it supports the incorporation of principles of branding into your life, while fostering an honest journey through your own self-actualization. It's a sort of spiritual journey, one that nudges you to unravel your greatest existence by discovering and maximizing your fullest potential. I've found that both the most challenging and rewarding elements of personal branding remain the discovery of clarity around the beliefs you hold about yourself: the truths you carry around who you are, what's unique about you, what has importance to you, and what motivates you to do the things you do.

Personal branding through "on-purpose" living forces you into being self-aware as you embrace your seed of authenticity: the overarching wiring of your life. It assists you in identifying what you're committed to doing and why you're motivated to do it. In exploring what values you hold dear, ask yourself these questions: How do I view myself? What kind of person do I want to be? What legacy do I want to create? Would you benefit from more schooling, experience, discipline—or belief in yourself? The ideal life of success and fulfillment looks different for everyone, and this is what makes authenticity, uniqueness, and diversity so powerful.

Being self-aware is more than being conscious of your own wiring. It's inclusive of understanding and directing your own energy, the vibes you send out, and recognizing the way you leave others feeling after they've interacted with you. Your core values, beliefs, and needs serve as the guiding forces behind your behaviors, personality, and overall ability to connect with others. In identifying what's authentic about your brand, use strong language with yourself that truthfully expresses how you view your most ideal self. Then yield to your personal ambitions as the driving force behind making life decisions reinforcing that self. Ask yourself, does this decision support who I am, who I'm working to become, the goals for my life, and the ideals I support? Always fall back on the behaviors that strengthen your brand and push you toward your next level of brilliance. Say yes only to the people, causes, and things that line up with the idea of the brand you're building, the mark you're making, and the legacy you're committed to leaving.

The way you view yourself and the contributions you make in the world are influential in determining your own value system, building confidence, and defining what you believe you can further accomplish in your life. I know that seems simple enough, but fear, frustrations, and prior disappointments all have an unfair way of robbing you of your vision and diligent focus, both of which are mandatory in realizing your greatest potential.

When you strive to build a business or work in an organization with a value system or culture that doesn't line up with your own, that effort will turn out to be unproductive or at minimum, stifling. Now, whether you should build your personal brand for short-term success or around the long-term goals of your career and dreams is certainly something to consider. In corporate branding, most teams aim to achieve both through strategic planning. As a personal brand, I believe you must balance the two. Allow your brand to create short-term awareness around where you are in your life, the value you're currently offering in your marketplace, and the people or causes you're serving.

Morgan, a twenty-four-year-old avid nature and animal activist, had the mission of finding a safe haven for every abandoned or lost dog on the streets of South Carolina's Lowcountry. Morgan worked for the Charleston Animal Society, passionately volunteered at Lowcountry

Animal Rescue, participated in fundraising efforts for adoptive services for pets, and dedicated her time to finding safe homes for abandoned dogs. Four years later, she found herself as mom to Dylan, the sweetest, fat-cheeked little boy east of the Copper River. In between work at the conservatory, Dylan's play dates, and managing her home, she developed a love for creating green parks in and around Charleston, South Carolina. It's not that Morgan's core values have changed, but her *priorities* have shifted to provide green spaces for Dylan to enjoy and explore nature. Her ideals remained intact; however, her contributions moved to align with her most immediate need.

You already have an genuine foundation, the core of who you are that motivates, gives meaning, drives, and inspires you to connect with the people, places, and things you're naturally drawn to. I believe in—and absolutely encourage you to embrace—the unconquerable power of living a passionate and purposeful life. You deserve nothing less. The cultivation and embrace of an authentic existence is the greatest gift you can give yourself—living, working, and building a brand that supports your own dreams and ideals. Why?

Because building your "on-purpose" brand unleashes personal power through the following:

- Directing you to clarify your values and the things you're great at.
- Setting short- and long-term goals in your life.
- Building your personal and professional network to match your core values, capabilities, passion, and persona.
- Distinguishing you from your competition, the other people who offer similar experience and expertise in your field. Humans are wired to recognize differences and have preferences.
- Educating people around what to expect when working or connecting with you.
- Demonstrating your specialty to gain credibility.
- Collaborating with people whose values, interests, passions, or ideals are similar to yours (like-minded individuals).

- Connecting emotionally and engaging with your target market or audience.
- Building confidence, trust, and pride in yourself and your work.
- Being inspired and motivated to make an impact on a larger scale.

In embracing your authenticity, keep in mind the needs, wants, and desires of the people you aim to serve: your target market. For example, the human resources director in a large accounting firm may be in the market for a junior accountant with the ability to learn consistently in a fast-paced environment, pay great attention to detail, and have strong organizational skills. The firm desires a great communicator who is social and comfortable speaking to their clients about accounting in English and Spanish. Meanwhile, you may be interested in a senior accountant consulting role within an organization, where you can utilize your entrepreneurial spirit, leadership, and effective business-development history. You can't—and shouldn't—try to be everything to everybody. Embracing your authenticity directs you to focus and hone in on what you want to be known for, to specialize in, or become an expert at.

Spend time becoming intimate with what your personal needs are not only for now but also in the future. Your needs will evolve as you grow, accomplish goals, and gain experience. It's important to remember that they'll always drive the core of your character and consequently direct your behaviors. A simple way to identify your personal needs, now and in the future, is to pinpoint the things for which you seek validation. As humans, our psychological wiring is very personal; it serves both the way we see ourselves and the things we perceive as meaningful and important. Accordingly, when the ways our lives play out doesn't align with our ideals, we often find ourselves out of balance and stagnant.

During my graduate-school studies, my interests and curiosity for theories behind persuasion, language, and resonance in marketing communication messages led me to delve into Maslow's theory and research on the hierarchy of needs. The basis of his theory has a influence on the way I approach branding. Abraham Harold Maslow in his 1943 paper, *A Theory of Human Motivation*.

The famous psychologist was eager to understand human motivation. He believed that every individual is powered by a different set of needs. The theory suggests some people have dominant needs at a particular level, and when those needs aren't met, they can't move up to the next level of hierarchy.

The five levels of need are presented in the illustration above, with the largest and most fundamental needs on the bottom tier and the need for self-actualization at the top.

The tiers are as follows from the bottom up:

PHYSIOLOGICAL NEEDS
This level of need tackles the basic necessities of human survival, like food, shelter and clothing. If a person doesn't fulfill these basic survival needs, he or she will have difficulty functioning.

SAFETY NEEDS
After the first level is met a person feels the need to have a life of security, where safety in all aspects of life is ensured.

SOCIAL NEEDS
This is our innate human need to feel as if we belong in a chosen social group and in beneficial relationships. This is the need for acceptance and affiliation. A deficiency here can lead to depression and loneliness.

ESTEEM NEEDS
This layer is the need to feel good about yourself and receive recognition from others. A lack here can lead to an inferiority complex and a sense of helplessness.

SELF-ACTUALIZATION
This layer addresses the need to become the best one can become. It personifies the need to maximize one's human potential.

Personal branding is most effective when initiated during the social, esteem, or self-actualization levels. Once your basic and immediate needs are met, and you're bursting at the seams to share your sacred seed of authenticity with others.

IDENTIFYING YOUR CORE VALUES (IDEALS)
The first step in defining your authenticity is to allow your innate values to guide you through the framing of your sense of purpose and the goals you desire for your life.

YOUR CORE VALUES
Take some time to reflect over what intimately resonate with you from the list below. Check the values that are most relevant to you. Then, circle back to choose your top two or three values.

Achievement: A feeling of mastery and accomplishment
Activity: Consistent and active work
Advancement: Growth and promotion
Adventure: Exciting and challenging opportunities

Aesthetics: Appreciation for the beauty in things
Affiliation: Involvement and association with others; belonging
Authority: Power to control
Autonomy: Working independently; self-sufficiency
Balance: The opportunity to have time for yourself, family, and community involvement
Challenge: Facing demanding tasks and issues
Change: Unpredictability and continual setting variation
Collaboration: Having cooperative working relationships with others
Community: Supporting people and causes that support a group of people living in the same place; having something in common
Competency: Demonstrating a lot of knowledge and proficiency
Competition: Contention to win
Courage: Inclination to stand up for your beliefs
Creativity: Uncovering new ideas and embracing imagination
Diversity: Inclusive ideas and perspectives
Enjoyment: Fun and joy
Harmony: Happiness, fulfillment, and contentment
Helping: Providing support and care to help others achieve their goals
Influence: Having an impact on the opinions of others
Justice: Equality and fairness
Loyalty: Faithfulness to others
Personal Development: Maximizing one's potential
Recognition: Public credit
Responsibility: A sense of accountability and dependability
Self-Respect: Self-esteem and personal identity
Significance: A sense of importance or meaning
Security: Steady and secure employment; financial stability
Spirituality: The use of prayer, meditation, or stillness to grow inner connectivity to something greater
Strategy: A sense for a deliberate and tactical approach

If you need assistance narrowing your list, complete the following exercise in your personal branding journal to help you uncover your deepest core values:

- Compile a list of your favorite people: professors, family members, friends, leaders, public figures, or celebrities. Which of their values resonate with you?
- Make another list of things that make you feel extremely happy and fulfilled while or after you participate in them. What values are being exercised that transpires into the feeling of happiness and fulfillment?
- When you're working on a project or doing things in your professional or personal life, what do you want people to recognize or say about you?
- For a moment, fast-forward to your retirement dinner. Imagine being surrounded by your family, friends, and colleagues as you're being honored for your career and legacy. What would you want them to say about you or your body of work?

The values you choose are emotional characteristics of your identity that embody the expressive currency of your life and give you meaning around things. They represent the personalized standards that drive your behavior, beliefs, attitude, choices, and preferences.

Your core values run your emotional circuitry, and everything you process is interrelated to them. No matter what situations you encounter in life, work to keep your values intact. You're wired the way you are, and you have a unique set of circumstances and traits that will lead you to brilliance—but you've got to do the work and commit to being the person you're aspiring to become. As you face challenging situations, let them provoke you to further fortify your values to reinforce your authenticity. In every problem, there are solutions of promise and possibilities that are much larger than the issue. In remaining true to yourself, you'll uncover fresh resolutions that'll build your confidence musculature and expose the will power you already had.

YOUR CAPABILITIES

The second step in defining your authenticity is combining the knowledge you've acquired, the skills you've developed, your innate talents, and your personal strengths to identify your best capabilities. Those rational proficiencies you've mastered: your strengths, abilities, and expertise. They play a dominant role in showing the world what's unique about you.

To help you identify your own strengths, I recommend the Gallup Organization's research project around the functions people perform. Gallup summarized the research into 34 strengths referred to as *Strengths-Finder qualities*. Once you review the list and identify themes that resonate with you; you can take identifying your own themes a step further and purchase the book Strengths-Finder 2.0 by Tom Rath (Gallup Press). The book provides a code in the back that takes you to www.strengthsfindercenter.com to take an online assessment that instantly reveals your top five themes.

In your journal in the back, write down your top five themes and two to three sentences on how they resonate with you. Use the themes and words from their description to create your personal brand statement in Chapter 5.

Achiever: A constant need for achievement. You must constantly achieve something tangible in order to feel good about yourself.

Activator: Once a decision is made you have to act. "When can we start?" This is a recurring question in your life. You make things happen.

Adaptability: You respond willingly to the demands of the moment. You don't view the future as a fixed destination.

Analytical: "Prove it. Show me why what you're claiming is true." You insist that theories be sound. You view yourself as objective and dispassionate. You like data because they are value-free.

Arranger: You are a conductor. When faced with a complex situation involving many factors, you enjoy managing all of the variables, aligning and realigning them until you are sure you have arranged them in the most productive configuration possible.

Belief: You have certain core values that are enduring. These core values give your life meaning and satisfaction; in your view, success is more than money and prestige. Your values provide you direction through life.

Command: You take charge. You feel no discomfort with imposing your views on others. On the contrary, once your opinion is formed, you need to share it with others.

Communication: You like to explain, to describe, to host, to speak in public and write. Ideas are a dry beginning. You feel a need to bring them to life, to energize them, to make them exciting and vivid.

Competition: Competition is rooted in comparison. When you look at the world, you are instinctively aware of other people's performance. Their performance is the ultimate yardstick.

Connectedness: You are sure things happen for a reason. In your soul you know that we are well connected. You gain confidence from knowing that we are not isolated from one another or from the earth and the life of it.

Consistency: Balance is important to you. You are keenly aware of the need to treat people the same, no matter what their station in life, so you do not want to see the scales tipped too far in any one person's favor. To you this leads to selfishness and individualism.

Context: You look back because you believe that is where the answers lie. You look back to understand the present.

Deliberative: You are a private, careful, and vigilant persona. You know that the world is an unpredictable place. Everything may seem in order, but beneath the surface you sense the many risks.

Developer: You see potential in others. Often, potential is all you see. In your view no individual is fully formed.

Discipline: Your world needs to be predictable. It needs to be ordered and planned. You instinctively impose structure on your world. You set up routines. You focus on timelines and deadlines.

Empathy: You can sense the emotions of those around you. You can feel what they are feeling as though their feelings are your own.

Focus: "Where am I headed?" you ask yourself. You ask this question every day. You need a clear destination. Lacking one, your life and work can quickly become frustrating.

Futuristic: "Wouldn't it be great if…" You love to peer over the horizon. The future fascinates you. As if it were projected on the wall, you see in detail what the future might hold, and this detailed picture keeps pulling you forward, into tomorrow.

Harmony: You look for areas of agreement. In your view, there is little to be gained from conflict and friction, so you seek to hold them to a minimum.

Ideation: You are fascinated by ideas. You're delighted when you discover beneath the complex surface an elegantly simple concept to explain why things are the way they are.

Includer: "Stretch the circle wider." This is the philosophy around which you orient your life. You want to include people and make them feel part of the group.

Individualization: You are intrigue by the unique qualities of each person. You are impatient with generalizations or "types" because you don't want to obscure what is special and distinct about each person.

Input: You are inquisitive. You collect things. You might collect information- words, facts, books, and quotations- or you might collect tangible objects such as butterflies or baseball cards. You collect what interests you.

Intellection: You like to think. You enjoy mental activity. You're introspective and enjoy time to think.

Learner: You love to learn. You'll always be drawn to the process of learning. You are energized by the steady and deliberate journey from ignorance to competence.

Maximizer: Excellence, not average, is your measure. Taking something from below average to slightly above average takes a great deal of effort and in you your opinion not very rewarding. Transforming something strong into something superb takes just as much effort but is much more thrilling.

Positivity: You are generous with praise, quick to simile, and always on the lookout for the positive in the situations. People want to be around you.

Relator: You are drawn towards people you already know. You do not necessarily shy away from meeting new people- in fact, you may have other themes that cause you to enjoy the thrill of turning strangers into friends. Still you derive a great deal of pleasure and strength from being around your close friends.

Responsibility: You take psychological ownership for anything you commit to, and whether large or small, you feel emotionally bound to follow it through to completion.

Restorative: You love to solve problems. You enjoy the challenge of analyzing the symptoms, identifying what is wrong, and finding the solution.

Self-Assurance: In the deepest part of you, you have faith in your strengths. You know that you are able: able to take risks, meet new challenges, to stake claims, and most important, able to deliver. You have confidence in both your abilities and your judgment.

Significance: You want to be very significant in the eyes of other people. In the truest sense of the word you want to be recognized. You want to be heard and you want to stand out.

Strategic: You are able to sort through the clutter and find the best route. It is not a skill that can be taught. It is a distinct way of thinking, a special perspective on the world at large.

Woo: Woo stands for winning over others. You enjoy the challenge of meeting new people and getting them to like you. Strangers are rarely intimidating to you. On the contrary, strangers can be energizing. You are drawn to them.

YOUR PERSONAL BRAND ATTRIBUTES

The third step in defining your authenticity is discovering your brand's persona and correlating voice. In corporate branding, giving each brand a persona helps consumers associate the product or service with distinct characteristics that specifically resonate with their target market. Similar to branding professionals, you're charged with understanding the emotional needs of your target, so you can communicate to them through messages that appeal to those needs. Within your brand's attributes are the emotional values you project—your personality, image, brand affiliations, and the overarching behaviors that emotionally connect you with others.

Reflect on personality attributes of larger-than-life celebrity brands we admire:

- Oprah Winfrey
- Ellen DeGeneres
- Michelle Obama
- Your favorite *The Real Housewives* cast member
- Beyoncé
- Matthew McConaughey
- Lady Gaga

Whether you've ever met the public figure or not, the things that come to mind were shaped by their brand's emotional and rational values, the people they serve, and what you believe they stand for. Think about your own brand now. What emotional and rational values do people appreciate about you? Are they the attributes you want to lead your brand? If not, why not? Either way, people have formed the same type of perceptions about your personal brand. In order to best shape those opinions about who you are and what you represent, you must consider the general public's current perception of you. Again, you can't control how others view you, but you can control the things you do to assure your behaviors support what you believe about yourself. Willfully accept or work at reshaping the attributes and reputation you don't take ownership of. While embracing the process of honing, openly expressing, and communicating the ones you do accept.

From the list of personality attributes below, circle those that best represent you.

- **Aggressive**
- **Assertive**
- **Captivating**
- **Charismatic**
- **Compassionate**
- **Competitive**
- **Confident**

- Confrontational
- Consistent
- Creative
- Demanding
- Direct
- Dominant
- Dynamic
- Emotional
- Empathetic
- Friendly
- Funny
- Hardworking
- Honest
- Humble
- Idealistic
- Intelligent
- Insightful
- Innovative
- Juvenile
- Kind
- Nurturing
- Opinionated
- Optimistic
- Passionate
- Practical
- Provocative
- Quiet
- Rational
- Reliable
- Reserved
- Scholarly
- Skeptical
- Strategic
- Tactical

- **Tenacious**
- **Thoughtful**
- **Trustworthy**
- **Vocal**
- **Warm**
- **Witty**
- **Youthful**

From the attributes you've chosen, narrow your selection down to your top three. In your branding journal in the back, construct a short paragraph about each of the traits. Describe why each personality attribute is relevant to you and why you own it. If I've left off an attribute that resonates with you more than the ones listed, add it. Spend a few minutes really thinking about this. If you were to select an actor or actress to portray you in your life's story five years from now, who would you choose to portray you? Why? What story would your biography tell? What's your dream car, house, or city? Why? What need do you have that owning that particular car or house will meet? What is it about that city that echoes with you? If you acquire the amount of money you believe would bring you career freedom and financial success, what would you do with the excess? Why?

YOUR PASSIONS

The forth and final step in defining your authenticity is identifying and supporting the things you're passionate about. Connecting with your passion is a great way for your creative thinking to express itself. Your passions provide you with an outlet to illustrate your commitment and enthusiasm toward causes or interests that are dear to you. In order to incorporate passion into your personal brand, first identify where the meat of your passion lies. What desires are directly connected to your heartstrings that represent things you undeniably enjoy?

Passion fuels creative energy into your life through the zest that lives within it. Has this ever happened to you? On a day you felt completely drained, exhausted, and with nothing left to give, someone called you to do something you're insanely passionate about. Did you miraculously perk up and find the energy to do it? When we engage in things in which we find joyful, it revitalizes our soul, gets our creative energy flowing, and raises our personal energy level. Leaving me to believe, you should engage in as many passion-filled experiences as humanly possible, all while avoiding falling into a job, career, or worse, a life that you're not passionate about. To prevent that trap, remain diligent at making career, business, and personal moves that reinforce your ability to thrive, find fulfillment, and move in the direction towards your dreams.

You only have a set amount of hours and energy to give within a day. With those limitations you should strategically decide which things you're going to dedicate your efforts to. Allow your interests of passion to guide you in making those very personal decisions about how to spend your free time. This may sound selfish, but really it's the most selfless thing you can do. With immense resistance from me, motherhood has shown me we're only as valuable as the energy we exude. When you're drained, frustrated, or experiencing any other feeling of deficit, you reflect that on those around you. You can't give something (energy included) you don't have to begin with. On the flip side, when you take care of yourself and feed your own needs, you evoke positive energy and vibrancy to share with those around you. Your passions are exclusively yours to invigorate your soul, feed your spirit, and invite joy into your life. The more often you fuel your passion, the happier you'll become.

Consider ways in which you can begin to integrate your passion into your own brand. Think about familiar celebrities and public figures whose careers are fueled by their passion. Steve Harvey and Kevin Hart's brands have built empires around humor. Although very different, both brands revolve around tummy-aching laughs, empowering themselves and others, outworking the competition, and using their voices to leverage philanthropic causes they care about. From his early days of doing stand-up to his popular syndicated radio and television shows—The Steve Harvey Morning Show, the Steve Harvey talk show, Little Big Shots, and Family Feud—Harvey built his fortune. Steve's brand uses his own rags-to-riches story to positively influence other people to reach for their own potential. He shares his life's lessons, time, and resources through his philanthropic foundation, The Steve and Marjorie Harvey Foundation. Steve Harvey has not only realized his dreams but also built an iconic, on-purpose brand around his capabilities and his passion for knowing how to make others laugh, in spite of whatever is happening around them. Your interests or passions can represent your signature persona or the mark of your brand.

In your branding journal, jot down two or three interests or activities that you are most passionate about. What activities get your emotions all fired up? What could you get lost in doing all day? Maybe there are things you did for hours as a kid during playtime or discovered a love for in college. After you've written them down, think of creative ways that'll encourage you to engage them in your weekly life.

With the self-awareness exercises you've completed around the four elements of authenticity you've identified use them to create you personal brand profile and personal brand statement in Chapter 5.

4

Your Secret Branding Weapon:
Mastering Effective Communication

Life isn't about finding yourself. Life is about creating yourself.

—George Bernard Shaw

Any good conversation requires the effective exchange and sharing of thoughts and ideas. In order to engage in a mutually successful dialogue, all parties have to express interest by listening, and then responding in a way that allows the other to know their thoughts and ideas are being transferred—not necessarily agreed with, but certainly *heard*. In this chapter, I'm providing more communication insight than you may need right now (or possibly ever). It's my hope you'll be able to use the content in years to come, as you continue to make your mark and build your brand.

With clarity around who you are, what you stand for, and those you serve, you're charged to effectively message your brand's story to the people who would benefit most from knowing you. Regardless of what field you're in, learning to successfully communicate your thoughts, ideas, and perspectives in a cohesive manner will support you in progressing your agenda in both your professional and personal life.

The art of communicating is the proficiency of gathering, evaluating, organizing, and disseminating information from a sender to a receiver. It's your ability to share your thoughts and feelings in a way that is understood by others. How effectively you do or don't communicate affects everything in your life—all the relationships you form, your career success, and the impact of influence you'll have on others. Often the biggest variable in your ability to communicate your messages efficiently is your use of words and body language in conjunction with the vibe (energy) you give off. Each component aiding your receiver in processing the message you're sending. I often hear people complaining that personal communication is a lost art. I see where the idea comes from with our wide use of social media engagement and text messaging, lending itself to people having fewer face-to-face or voice interactions. With less personal interactions, there is a loss of using your body language and energetic vibes to reinforce the messages you're sending. The ability to communicate in layman's terms with simplicity is highly regarded in branding, so make it your goal: clear, concise, relevant, and then repeat.

How many times has this happened to you? You say something or send a text or an e-mail that was so completely misinterpreted, it threw you for a loop. It happens to me. I get the less-than-desirable response, take a deep breath, and either laugh or take a few more breaths. I've learned not to immediately go sideways and instead try to see where the miscommunication happened. Usually at some point, I'll get to a giggle. Eventually, I'll clarify my intention. Communicating in the digital era has become more challenging than ever before. It's not that the English language has changed, but technology and the wide use of jargon have certainly changed the landscape of the dialogue. They continue to create more communication short cuts. Personal example: if you have a teenager, you certainly know what WYD (What you doing?) and IKR (I know, right?) mean.

"Less is more" is certainly the way to communicate when you're attempting to keep people engaged and interested in what you have to say. That's in everything from engaging in small talk to delivering a keynote address. Our society is oversaturated with messages, data, and noise on a daily basis. If you want to be heard, be clear, concise, and relevant.

Learning to tell your story in a succinct and interesting way is a prized weapon branding. Every day, you send verbal and nonverbal messages that are translated into the perceptions others form about you. Consider a colleague who storms into your office in the morning. Her eyes are slightly swollen, even a tad watery. There are traces of mascara on her nose. You notice her blood-orange cheeks as she kicks her purse under her cubicle and sinks into her chair. Minutes later, you ask her if everything is okay. After she ignores you for a few seconds, she looks up with tears and replies, "Yes, I'm fine." Would you believe what she verbalized to you (her words) or would you believe her nonverbal communication (her tone and behavior)? Most people would believe the nonverbal message, as body language may reveal more about what a person is thinking and feeling than verbal communication does.

NONVERBAL COMMUNICATION

As you consciously guide your brand, keep in mind your words are more than the sum of their parts. They're not delivered in bits and pieces, your receiver will carry away an overall impression from the words you say, the memory of the dialogue as a whole. Nonverbal communication refers to the components of communication aside from the actual words you use to express yourself. Measures of nonverbal communication include how your body moves, how pleasant to uninterested your face appears, and your use of open versus closed posture. Open postures include those stances in which your body faces toward the person you're engaging while sitting or standing up straight with your head raised. Closed postures include sitting in a slouched position, clenching your fists, crossing your legs away from someone, crossing your arms at your chest, holding your head down, or looking away from your subject.

From a psychological standpoint, open postures are associated with a measure of receptivity, closeness, and even interest. Using them illustrates positive feelings toward others or the subject matter. On the other hand, closed postures traditionally indicate defensiveness, detachment, and avoidance. In general, approach your conversations and speeches with body language that is open and inviting. Try to avoid the use of closed body poses; they may be perceived as a negative feeling toward the topic or person with whom you're interacting. Think about it, when someone crosses or folds his or her arms high, looks down when speaking, fidgets with things, or appears otherwise uncomfortable when speaking with you, how does that make you feel?

Much of the research on nonverbal communication indicates that as little as 7 percent of communication is spoken; the vast majority are nonverbal, paralinguistic cues. When you send contradicting messages, people will tend to believe the predominant nonverbal communication over your verbal one. So remain mindful of not just what you're saying but how you say it. That's as important or more in some cases. Since practice makes perfect, begin to practice applying positive nonverbal signals when communicating with others.

COMMUNICATING IS A CONTACT SPORT

Communicating what you represent as a brand is more complex than a handshake and exchange of names. Your ability to convey what you have to say directly impacts the influence your brand will garner. With that in mind, work to express your brand story confidently, succinctly, and persuasively. It's not a secret the most successful people in any given industry are either the most talented or the most effective marketers and communicators. Why? Undeniably, talent speaks for itself. Great marketers are great communicators who know how to capture, engage, and connect with people. Communication is a contact sport, so do it early and often. We've all been impressed by the incredible impact of effective communications and how it drives influence and positive impact for personal brands in our digital era. With a few communication best practices to lead your efforts, you can certainly communicate with the best of them. As with anything, it may seem intimidating at first, but done consistently, it'll become so familiar, you'll get comfortable with it.

FIRST IMPRESSIONS

You've heard it before, but never have first impressions been more important than in building your brand. Not only does what you say matter, but also how you say it, the body language you use, and the vibe you give off form lasting impressions. You get how important they are, but do you know you only have a few seconds for an impression to be formed? A first impression can often be impossible to reverse, making that initial encounter critical. It sets the tone for the relationship. Whether for your career or social life, it's important to establish strong first impressions.

When making solid first impressions, consider the following:

- The moment someone sees you, his or her brain makes a thousand assessments. Are you someone to approach or avoid? Are you friendly or not? Do you have authority or not? Are you trustworthy and competent or not?
- Although our initial assessments of others are formed at our subconscious level, we use that subconscious processing to direct the perceptions we form about one another.
- In professional interactions, first impressions are crucial. No, you can't stop people from making judgmental decisions. The human brain is hardwired in this way as a prehistoric survival mechanism. So make those imprints work in your favor.
- First impressions are heavily influenced by nonverbal cues. Studies have found that nonverbal cues have on average four times the impact of verbal cues on the impression you make.

Knowledge is power. Empower yourself to be approachable to others. Greet them with a smile, good posture, clear communication, and strong eye contact.

CONFIDENCE

Before educating others about who you are and those you're committed to serving, you need to believe in yourself, your abilities, and the power of possibilities that are inherent in your life. Your own beliefs must give you the assurance to purposely embrace your life and blaze your own unique voyage to realizing your highest potential. The more self-awareness you gain around your capabilities, attributes, talents, and overall value, the stronger your confidence will develop. While the more prepared you approach a task the more confidence you'll have about it.

Self-confidence plays a critical role in our lives; impacting not just our business success but all the interactions we have in our personal lives. And to be clear, make sure you understand the difference between *confidence* and *arrogance*.

Arrogance is the manifestation of self-doubt, an outward expression of inadequacy. It's point-blank offensive and should be avoided at all cost. Confidence, on the other hand, is your ability to feel good about yourself and what you bring into the world. It translates as a presence of poise and self-assuredness that directs others to perceive you as comfortable in the skin you're in. When you understand your own uniqueness, the value it presents, and the brilliance you have to share, your confidence rises. To come across as confident (even when you may be feeling anything but in the moment), stand tall, hold your head high, roll your shoulders back, give strong eye contact, and balance your breathing.

Confidence, even among experts, can waver. It's natural to find yourself confident at one thing but not so confident at other things. The key is to practice projecting confidence until you master it. The more you prove to yourself that you're an authentic, valuable, capable, evolving, and malleable being, the more confidence musculature you'll build.

Studies suggest confidence is one of the top characteristics both men and women find the most attractive in one another. It's considered more important than skill, knowledge, or experience to some hiring managers. Confidence can set you apart from others, sometimes even more qualified candidates. According to one study, portraying confidence translates into you being competent. There is no doubt; your level of confidence plays a major role in how far you'll go in pursuit of your life goals. As it's often said, a successful person was afraid and did it anyway, while the unsuccessful person allowed fear to stop him. I believe fear is the biggest dream stealer of all times; ironically, often it overpromises and underdelivers. But just how do you build the confidence you need to muster the courage to pursue your professional and personal brand goals?

To strengthen your confidence, stay extremely mindful and appreciative of the things in your life in which you've already found success. It's been proven that simple activities like exercising frequently and wearing perfume boosts your self-confidence. Research shows that in addition to thinking positively, spritzing on your favorite scent, surrounding yourself with emotional support, setting and accomplishing goals, and exercising regularly all boost confidence. Most of us have experienced the positive effects of a great butt-kicking workout. You know the one—when you think you're going to die from exhaustion right before those endorphins start kicking in. But in no time, like magic, you receive a surge of energy. The same mood-enhancing effect plays a direct role in increasing your positive perception of yourself—and that drives confidence.

Amy Cuddy, a social psychologist and professor at Harvard Business School, found that the students most actively involved in their classroom setting were inclined to display power poses: open, more dominant positions, their arms out and heads up. On the other hand, quieter students showed a tendency to sit in closed positions, their hands folded and heads down. Cuddy and her fellow researchers pondered if a conscious shift to more dominant poses would change internal confidence indicators. As it turns out, they did. By having research participants take on power poses for just two minutes, they recorded an increase in testosterone, a decrease in cortisol, and an increase in risk-taking behaviors. In a correlating TED (Technology, Entertainment, Design) talk Cuddy goes on to share a way we can change both how we feel about ourselves and how others perceive us—by spending two minutes "power posing" with our chins lifted, our arms or elbows out, with an expansive posture. The research indicates that by taking on the body language of dominance for as little as 120 seconds our bodies can produce a 20 percent increase in testosterone (the dominance hormone) and a 25 percent decrease in cortisol (the stress hormone). This made me wonder what would happen if, prior to that job interview, meeting, or networking event, you made the effort to take on a power pose and reap the benefits of increased confidence. It's documented that a confident smile can be more attractive than good looks, according to research out of Webster University and as reported in *Time* magazine. When Dr. Monica Moore studied flirting techniques in bars and malls to see which ones worked best, she found that it wasn't necessarily the most physically attractive people who got approached the most, it was the ones who made eye contact and smiled with confidence.

PUBLIC SPEAKING

I remember as if it were only yesterday. As an intimidated freshman at Morgan State University, I bashfully found myself in a public-speaking class with a gang of upperclassmen. (Let's be clear: one of the hottest guys on Morgan State University's campus in 1994 happened to be a part of the group.) I was born in Maryland, but I grew up in Shulerville, South Carolina, so I inherited a cute (to other folks, not so much to me as a communications major) southern drawl. As if my distinctive southern accent wasn't distracting enough, I spoke really fast when I became nervous. The first two weeks of speech class, I found myself a hot mess. Reluctantly, I began to accept that I may very well bomb my speeches and become the laughingstock of class. Then something interesting transpired: I became mesmerized by my professor's seamless ability to make speech delivery appear so natural. Things gradually took a pleasant turn for me, and throughout the semester, I eventually looked forward to giving my keynotes. No question, my respect for public speaking was certainly born from fear, determination, and an appreciation for the power in the use of words, intonation, and rhetoric to garner command.

Public speaking is an ideal outlet and useful platform to help you accelerate your overall brand, both on- and offline. Certainly, polishing your speaking delivery is a process you'll continue to perfect the rest of your career. The sooner you make yourself available for speaking opportunities, the quicker it'll become comfortable for you. With every speaking experience under your belt, you'll gain more confidence and tips, and as a result, naturally strengthen your ability for the next opportunity.

Many people shy away when they're asked to deliver a speech or address a group. They're afraid of not knowing what to say, forgetting what to say, stumbling over their words, or at baseline, looking or sounding crazy. Fair enough, not to mention, early in your career you may not have considered ever making a speech. It may not have crossed your mind why an accountant, dentist, or an artist may need to acquire public-speaking skills. Yet speaking in front of an audience is a way of life for many leaders, influencers, and career professionals across all industries.

More often than not, professionals with influence find themselves being asked to present their perspectives, ideas, and areas of expertise to other people in a public setting. Being competent as an effective public speaker is a beneficial resource to have along your personal branding journey, and there are basic principles you can apply. Before delivering your speech, choose an appropriate topic, and identify what you're looking to gain from your audience. Frame your delivery as it relates to the response you'd like to get; provide enough evidence to support the assertions you're making. Make sure to run through logical ways of reasoning in your delivery, to aid you in presenting your ideas in a sound and persuasive manner. Through speaking in a tone that's appealing to your audience, with a clear sense of purpose, they'll understand what they're expected to do, believe, or think.

Practice your speeches in front of a mirror. It's a helpful exercise that'll help you see what your audience will see; not to mention, there is something about practicing over and over again that aids your brain in absorbing more of the information so you can recall it easier. Most of your public-speaking opportunities will come with parameters regarding the amount of time you'll have to deliver your masterpiece. It's refreshing for your audience when you appeal to them emotionally. To build that resonance, weave personal experiences and insight throughout your talk; consider things of personal relevance like your education, career experience, organizational affiliations, travels, memorable childhood experiences, hobbies, and the people or books you find inspirational.

ORGANIZING YOUR SPEECH

Let's look at how using an organizational structure can enhance your speaking style. According to Plato, "Every discourse ought to be a living creature, having a body of its own and a head and feet; there should be a middle, beginning, and end, adapted to one another and to the whole." Following Plato's philosophy, organize your speech by setting up a structure with the three basic parts of speeches: the introduction, the body, and the conclusion.

INTRODUCTIONS

Your speeches will be delivered to audiences with varying interest levels on the topic. First, make it your immediate priority to capture their attention. Next, build some initial credibility. Start by positioning your talk. Consider having your positioning phase communicate the purpose of your speech, establish credibility with the audience, and state the perspective or argument you're trying to reason. Observed together, the attention grabber and the positioning statement, prepare your audience to listen from a place of engagement: "Participating in a personal branding through "on-purpose" workshop is a great way to gift yourself with an accountability partner along your journey through self-actualization." That's a much stronger opening than "I'm here to remind you that you may be haphazardly going through your life without working toward measurable goals and career success." Your purpose should be clear as you speak directly to your audience. At this point, connect the dots for them as to why this is important information, why you're qualified to present it, and what perspective or stance you want them to have regarding the subject.

The more emotionally invested your audience becomes, the more credibility you'll build. Exactly how do you establish credibility with your audience? Consider sharing information about yourself that qualifies you to speak to as an authority on the topic you're covering.

Try these introductory, attention-grabbing techniques:

- **Establish common ground with the audience.** "Thank you for the warmth of your welcome back to Morgan State University. I refuse to feel old, although the last time I stood here I was young, wild, and naive. I owe a lot to Morgan. My mother, aunt, and sister attended this wonderful university. Not to mention that numerous friends and I began our careers in this dynamic city. I'm truly grateful to be back where it all connected for me."

- **Pay the audience an authentic compliment.** "I'm grateful to be back here where it all clicked for me in the '90s. I'm impressed by how innovative and gorgeous this campus is. The renovations are stunning, yet the university has protected its quaintness and overarching sense of family." Consider asking a rhetorical question that doesn't require an outward verbal or behavioral response; use it to stimulate thought and pique curiosity. Describe a hypothetical situation involving value judgment and then pose a thought-provoking question.

- **Nothing tickles the soul quite like humor.** If you're comfortable with humor, use it. Not everyone is funny, but if you are, use your funny side. People love to laugh.

- **Use a narrative or illustration that leads into the subject.** "Ladies and gentlemen of Morgan State, a trusted colleague working in media recently told me a typical interview on her radio show used to run twenty minutes. Today, it's condensed to ten minutes, still double the time of the average television evening news story. The average recording nowadays days lasts all of three to four minutes, or about the time it takes to read the publisher page of your favorite magazine. There tends to be one exception to this relentless compression of time in our fast-paced life: the graduation speech. Everyone still expects and respects that it takes time to deliver a message meant to inspire, motivate, and guide students for a lifetime."

THE SPEECH'S BODY

The body is where the magic happens. During the body of your speech, you'll deliver the meat (the good stuff/purpose) of your talk. The body should take up the majority of your speaking time. Have it disclose your subject's information and introduce your persuasive strategy.

Consider having your body structured in one of the following orders:

1. **Chronological** (in order of time)
2. **Spatial** (in order of location)

3. **Analytical** (in order of causes to effects)
4. **Topical** (in order of types, forms, and qualities of speech subject)
5. **Problem and Solution** (in order of problem to possible or best solutions)

If you opt for chronological order, begin with a given time and move forward or backward, depending on the subject and the structure you choose. If you choose spatial arrangement, use space as your ordering principle. Discuss your topics based on location, whether it's the geographical location in the world, nation, city, or town. When you deliver an analytical speech, consider choosing cause and effect, but make sure to address the problem (effect) as it relations to the contributing causes. In looking at a given effect to seek its causes, don't oversimplify. Normally there is more than one cause going into an effect. It's best to use this problem-and-solution technique when your audience is very familiar with the nature and causes of the problem. You may choose to briefly mention it, provide supporting factual information, and spend the remainder of your time exploring solutions. Discuss answers that permit the audience to choose which one they authentically believe in. If you have a preferred solution for the view of your corporation's or organization's standpoint or specific reasons you want your audience to support a selected option, your preparatory research should strongly support the preferred solution.

To avoid the trap of incoherence, provide your audience with unity and interrelatedness of the ideas you're presenting. This will serve to be helpful in creating links by revealing the talk's main ideas as an essential part of the whole speech. Have each idea transition smoothly into your next idea. Good transitions will ensure your speech moves with coherence and provides a smooth flow for your dialogue. In presenting each idea, bring that idea full circle before moving on to the next concept.

DRAWING CONCLUSIONS

Standing heartbeat to heartbeat, pupil to pupil with your audience, conclude your talk with a proposed solution as the best outcome to the issue you're discussing. Your conclusion presents the opportunity to bring your speech to a strategic close. Consider making your proposed conclusion based around the principles you've presented, backing the outcome you want your audience to do, believe, or support.

Aim to have your conclusion include reasoning. There are two basic types of reasoning that work well in wrapping your speech: inductive and deductive. Think of inductive reasoning as a way of drawing generalizations from a set of observations, from the particular to the general. Deductive reasoning is just the opposite. A deductive method of reasoning draws from general principles to form specific conclusions. This is very similar to stereotyping, the single most destructive, inductive fallacy alive.

Generally, people have numerous experiences with a limited number of people from a particular group. This leads them to automatically make assumptions about an entire group based on their experiences. Unfortunately, making hasty, premature conclusions about the characteristics of an entire group is a mistake too many people make. Using inductive reasoning, keep in mind no two people's perceptions are alike. Because of differences in their abilities, expectations, values, prior experiences, and the basis of their belief systems, perceptions are all highly individual. Research suggests that many of us unknowingly participate in selective perceptions and selective retention, both of which lead us to only recall certain parts of things perceived, and as a result, our memories can be distorted, filtered, or forgotten.

With that, keep in mind that selectivity is often unintentional; it happens in our subconscious minds. Selective perception and retention create difficulties with inductive reasoning, since the quality of our conclusion is only as effective as our perceived and remembered data. So, to reach a conclusion deductively, begin with a generally accepted idea or premise and apply it to a specific situation. As the opposite of inductive reasoning, the perceptions are broad. I'm guilty of this. If I believe an author is smart and progressive, I tend to buy every book he or she writes, even if the subject isn't of interest to me. The deductive thinker in me assumes that because the author is smart and progressive,

I need to know everything that he or she perceives. Both inductive and deductive reasoning leads us to conclusions that are probable rather than absolutely true. Is anything ever absolute?

Your friend Molly parties like an '80s rock star on the weekends, and as a result, more often than not, she's tired, late, and hungover on Monday mornings. Given what you know about Molly, you may deductively conclude that if you invite her to join your early Monday morning yoga class, she'll only make a few of them. This may be right, but your deduced conclusion could also be wrong.

SPEECH TOPICS

As you select appropriate speech topics, lean toward ones you already have a good deal of knowledge in and a genuine interest in learning more about. To garner influence, only speak about what you know about; gather sound evidence and reach logical conclusions to advance your argument or perspective. Contemplate subjects with regard to the demographic characteristics of your audience, their age, socioeconomic status, educational level, desires, or special interests. The more information you're equipped with regarding your audience, the easier it'll become for you to choose a topic that'll be professionally, personally, or socially significant for them. Select your topic with relevance, appropriateness for you and the audience, and your listeners' needs, values, and interests in mind. As you deliver your speech, both you and your audience should be engaged for meaningful two-way communication. Once it's over, your audience should be excited about what you want them to do.

Consider approaching your topic selection from the four categories:

1) **Audience**: It's a plus to choose a topic your audience is familiar with and is eager to learn more about.
2) **Personal:** Enlist the most interesting source of speech ideas from your personal experiences, knowledge, and beliefs. With each talk you deliver, share your personal statement about your topic, your experience, and your personal perspective on it.

3) **Situational**: On those occasions when you find yourself delivering a speech that could have an impact on the topic and have different meanings to the audience (especially if it is a celebration of an anniversary or victory, or in honor of a special achievement), be respectful and sensitive to those meanings.

4) **Organizational**: As you speak to an organizational group, if you must choose a subject with controversy, make sure to know the organization's stance on the topic. Find out if it has taken any opposing public stance. If so, research if the position is public knowledge. Consider the degree to which your personal views coincide with the organization's; if they do, discard the subject totally or deliver the speech in such style a variety of viewpoints emerge without identifying your own.

YOUR AUDIENCE'S PERSPECTIVE

Engaging speakers are expected to interest, entertain, inform, persuade, inspire, humor, motivate or instruct. You don't necessarily have to be an award-winning comedian, master teacher, or litigating attorney, but you must interject your personality and distinct energy to connect with your audience. If you're naturally funny, use your humor. Infuse your speech with your natural personality while bringing home your points.

INTEREST

Don't devalue the significance of interest. Simply because a speech provides actual information and well-heeled appeals, that's never a guarantee of success. Be mindful that ideas, information, and statistics should be related to the interests and needs of your audience. Your audiences must be engaged to learn, be moved, inspired, uplifted, or educated. Bottom line: master interest. Naturally there'll be a level of uncertainty in how much engagement each audience finds, but most people are interested in information they view as relevant, useful, startling, new, entertaining, or worth sharing. It's always a plus to pick topics your audience is familiar with and appreciates learning more about.

TO INFORM

Most likely the majority of speeches you'll deliver will be to inform others about something you already know a good deal about. As the messenger, your job is to impart and share information about the topic. From time to time, you'll present information that is totally new to the audience, but mostly you'll be expanding on topics they're already somewhat familiar with. Hence, you'll either offer a different perspective or interpretation on something the audience is already acquainted with or provide new statistics or discoveries.

When delivering an informative speech, your goal is to achieve audience understanding. Have your informative speech meet as many of the following standards as possible:

- Deliver meaningful points that align with your audience's interests, needs, and level of understanding.
- Provide precision through detailed research, study, and comprehension.
- Provide completeness by providing the most important elements to deliver a solid understanding of the subject.
- Create unity by conveying your content with clarity, concise thought progression, and adherence to the core theme of your topic.

Remember, informative speeches are meant to inform your audience first, but don't stop there. Interject your style and personality. Sharing the content of your speech is the means for building common ground around your subject matter. Whether or not persuasion is your ultimate goal, remain mindful; your style of information dissemination may influence your audience's perspective on the topic.

TO PERSUADE

The ability to persuade plays a major role in public speaking. While the degree to which you'll be expected to persuade your audience will vary: persuasion as a form of engagement, as a way to change someone's perspective, or as a technique to convince your audience to act in a particular way. Ideally, the audiences you'll address have values and interests similar to yours and support why you've been asked to deliver the talk. While some speeches are for the purpose of changing or influencing belief, provoking action, or exciting, more often than not, your audience will consist of people with mixed feelings toward your topic. Some members will be supportive, some may completely oppose your position, while others will be neutral to your perspective. Regardless, your goal is usually to persuade them to believe and buy into your proposition or interpretation. For some audiences, this calls for a significant change to their current beliefs. Changing people's minds is no easy task, as most of their beliefs are deeply rooted from their own personal experiences and values.

In your attempts to persuade your audience, some members may receive your insight positively. They will show appreciation for your delivery, its content, and the flow of information you provide—yet remain unaffected by your appeal. As a public speaker, you'll likely find yourself in the position to solicit votes, money, interest, support, and time commitments to show support to a cause, initiative, or movement. This isn't easy, but the more comfortable, confident, and at ease you become in moving folks into action, the more in demand you'll become as a speaker.

Consider using these tips when speaking to persuade others:

- Evaluate your audience; learn as much about them beforehand as possible.
- Build credibility with them early in your delivery.
- Appeal to their emotions.
- Use evidence in your speech that supports your claim.

CLEAR PURPOSE

To write a clear purpose for your speech, frame your ideas and provide information that supports each of your notions. Create a purpose statement to use as your guide in keeping your focus on content that aligns your message with supporting your purpose.

To create your speech's purpose statement, implement the following guidelines to help you find clarity in your thought process:

- **What is the primary goal for your speech?** Inspire? Entertain? Inform? Stimulate? Move your audience to act, change, or shape their perspective? What kind of audience understanding are you looking to gain? What are you going to do to be engaging? What degree of persuasion are you seeking?
- **What audience response are you looking for?** Do you want them to enjoy the speech? Understand a comparison? Learn something new? Open their minds to a different understanding? Do you want to convince them to act in a certain way?
- **Is your purpose obtainable?** Within the time frame you have, can you achieve your purpose? Is it a reasonable goal, given the knowledge of the audience's needs, desires, interests, values, and demographic characteristics?
- **Are you crystal clear on your purpose?** Is your purpose focused enough that you eliminate confusion with the audience? Is the content sufficient enough to support the audience response you are seeking?

PROVIDE EVIDENCE SUPPORTING YOUR SPEECH'S GOAL

Regardless of the goal for your speech, it's best to communicate various ideas, contentions, and propositions throughout it. Let's say that your goal is to have the audience donate funds for a nonprofit organization supporting after-school learning for children. You may assert, "The compassionate, caring, and charitable citizens residing at 54 West Loop can positively influence the trajectory of twenty kids at Friends Foundation by committing to be a part of their 20-Plus Movement." On the basis of this assertion alone, the audience won't know if that argument is weak or strong. To convince the audience the contention is sound, it must be supported with evidence; share statistics of the program's successes and the positive influences the program has had on past participants' lives.

Your evidence should consist of a body of both facts and opinions pertaining to the subject. When possible, use supporting visual aids. Include your evidence in the body of facts and opinions you state pertaining to the subject. Consider exploring different types of evidence like reports, research statistics, and specific examples.

Strive to make the majority of the evidence you present factual, but feel free to personalize your talk by including objective descriptions. If your view of reality is accurate and verifiable, it's factual. As you collect your factual data, use reliable, fact-checked sources. Look at multiple sources to discover consistent facts. Incorporating accurate statistical data is helpful; it provides a precise, numerical method to share convincing numbers of instances.

With the majority of your evidence consisting of facts, weave in your personal opinions, references, or experiences. Different types of opinions will carry different weight with your audience. Expert testimony is normally the most valuable, followed by personal and lay opinions. Aim to support your presentations with your interjection on the subject matter from time to time. The level of success you'll achieve in using your own opinion for support will largely depend on the credibility you've established with your audience. If your audience perceives you as being highly knowledgeable, intelligent, and accomplished in the subject area, and you appear trustworthy in your motives, your personal testimony will have weight. Regardless of your credibility, don't rely on that alone. It's always beneficial to share additional research, statistics, and examples to support your point.

Often, making general principles or abstract notions interesting and meaningful to an audience is challenging. To get around that, provide solid frames of reference and interject real-life examples to add meaning and resonance to the points you're making. Examples are easy for others to identify with, and they can be a powerful means of supporting your ideas. Use examples that support the general principle or assertions you're trying to make to build a clear connection between your example and the message you're delivering.

CHOOSING YOUR SPEECH DELIVERY

Whether you're asked to give a speech at a celebratory dinner, a work meeting, an organization's conference, or your best friend's wedding, there are basic strategies to implement in putting your "best word forward." You know there is more to giving speeches than the words you use and the outfit you plan to rock. Of course, your facts must be accurate and your wardrobe appropriate, but your message must be relevant and your delivery engaging. With that, there are four basic types of speech delivery: impromptu, extemporaneous, manuscript, and memorized.

Impromptu speeches are fairly easy, spur-of-the-moment talks delivered without preparation. Impromptu requests may be made of you during meetings, at a dinner, or during a social gathering. Whether being put on the spot at a friend's wedding, as a leader in your career, or among the communities you interact, you could be called upon for an "of-the-moment" speech. When asked to deliver an impromptu speech, you're being called on to articulate your point of view, make a brief reporting of some information, or explain something with which you're already familiar, so that should lend you confidence right there. Even when your speech is going to be short and impromptu, take a moment to organize and outline your thoughts. Remember to breathe slowly, keep your ideas brief and to the point, maintain strong eye contact, and speak at a conversational pace.

Extemporaneous speeches allow you to use a loose guideline with cues reminding you where you're going with your thoughts. When speaking extemporaneously, commit your key ideas to memory, but not the exact wording. Thoroughly outline and practice your speech. Only your specific phrases and connective examples should fluctuate from your practice sessions to the actual presentations. Use your notes as a reminder of the delivery strategy you've planned. Allow yourself to deviate from them when the situation calls for it. As with the other delivery methods, rehearse your speech for timing, rhythm, and a natural flow.

Once you've rehearsed your core concepts, take the opportunity to interject your personality throughout it. Your audience will always provide you cues into how they're absorbing your information. As an extemporaneous speaker, your willingness to make slight delivery adjustments in response to your audience's reaction will prove useful. If they appear very interested or entertained by something, elaborate more on that part of the delivery. Feed off their energy. If they look confused and appear lost, provide them more contextual clarity. If they're amused, incorporate more wit. A big part of delivering great extemporaneous speeches is in your ability to read the crowd and adjust to your audience's receptivity.

Manuscript speeches require you to write your speech word-for-word and read the manuscript to your audience. Although this sounds easy enough, you're not granted the flexibility to adapt to the feedback you get from your audience. Using the manuscript delivery is most common in conservative business settings. More often than not, the manuscript you'll be asked to deliver will be required from you ahead of time, to be approved by the group you'll be delivering to or on behalf of. Often, a manuscript is required when an organization or corporation's speaker is addressing a controversial topic or when the press may be present. The benefit of reading word-for-word offers you protection against missing words or leaving out important facts. Manuscript speaking provides the most precise delivery of the materials, but they absolutely must be conveyed with energy and momentum to keep the audience interested. No one wants to sit through a speech feeling like they've just been read a bedtime story. When presenting manuscript style, it's a nice gesture to provide your audience with copies of the manuscript so they may revisit it in detail later.

Memorized speeches require you to deliver your talk word-for-word and are very difficult. In delivering a memorized speech you're expected to memorize it and then deliver it without having it sound as though it's been memorized. I recommend leaving memorized speeches for professional speakers.

When given the ability to choose, opt for the delivery that best suits the organization and audience you're addressing. Whenever appropriate and when time permits, offering a brief question-and-answer session after your summary is a great engagement technique. Allow only a few questions, and offer a source of follow-up where those who still have questions can find out additional information. Simplicity provides the best clarity. Use simple words, avoid being pretentious, and don't overdo it with too many clichés.

Regardless of the topic you choose, strive for a strong delivery. Incorporating these tips will help you do so:

- Use personal pronouns (*you, we, ours,* and *yours*).
- Be knowledgeable regarding the content.
- Choose a topic you're genuinely interested in.
- Practice using an effective volume. Remain loud enough for everyone in the room to hear you, while not appearing to shout.
- Vary your tone, pitch, and speed so you don't sound monotonous.
- Aim for a casual, conversational voice.
- Use great eye contact throughout your delivery.
- Practice natural facial expressions, body language, and hand gestures; make sure they align with the ideas and feelings you're attempting to express.
- Use short sentences and simple words. Audiences don't carry dictionaries; don't try to impress them with big words they may not know. Use words and context that are instantly intelligible.
- Use rhetorical questions. They are good attention-getting techniques that can be used in your introduction, throughout the body of the speech, and even for your closing. Rhetorical questions grab attention because they challenge the audience to think.
- Seek to rouse the audience's imagination. Include figurative words by including metaphors, similes, repetition, and other figures of speech.
- Use repetition of words, key phrases, and ideas. Repetition is a great way to reinforce the things you want to share with your audience. When you're reading a great book, you have the luxury of going back and rereading content you like or need clarity on, but your audience can't rewind. Repetition is a way to reinforce your

key ideas, so consider using colorful expressions and slogans that will remain with your audience once the speech is over.

- Give your speech a conversational tone. Like in your daily conversations, use contractions (*I've, we can't,* or *she isn't,* rather than *I have, we cannot,* or *she is not*). Contractions make your speeches come across more natural and conversational.
- Rehearse, tweak, and rehearse until you're comfortable with the subject and your delivery of it.

OVERCOMING ANXIETY TO DELIVER YOUR SPEECH IN CONFIDENCE

Anxiety in public speaking is a very natural and common occurrence. In fact, professional speakers often experience anxiety before or during their delivery. One study suggests that 77 percent of all experienced speakers admitted to some stage fright prior to every speaking engagement. Some of the most eloquent orators of all time were besieged by stage fright. So, anxiety isn't infrequent; it's actually expected.

In most cases, your stage fright decreases as you gain more confidence and experience. As public speaking becomes a part of your life, you'll meet future assignments with greater confidence and proficiency. As a speaker, don't overrate how much your listeners are aware of your nervousness. Don't assume they can see through your calm and collected appearance; they won't—*as long as you remain in control.* The turmoil or anxiety that may lurk beneath the surface can certainly be contained. Your increased energy can manifest itself in shaking hands or other signs of nervousness. Anxiety is just a surge of unsettled energy, don't fight it use your adrenaline rush to go loud. Why not channel it into positive behaviors for a more creative and animated presentation? It's common for speakers to be overly sensitive of their presentation, thinking they appeared more nervous than the audience perceived them to be.

Psychological studies suggest moderate anxiety can be an asset to your performance when delivering a speech. Embrace the anxiety as a stimulus for a stronger performance. Moderate tension provides you with more creativity; channel that energy into an enthusiastic delivery.

In building your brand, know what you're speaking about. Collect sound and sufficient evidence to support your logical conclusions. Since the purpose of your talk is to impact and influence your audience about your topic, it's critical that your speech be memorable, leave a strong impression, and effectively bring home the message. I highly recommend two great techniques used in persuasive speeches: First, conclude with a challenge. Challenge your audience to act, believe, meet the need, demonstrate concern, or do something different. Second, when giving great information and persuasion speeches, use a summary conclusion, summarizing the main points of your message in a repetitive, clear, and literal way. Restate the major ideas in different ways. I tend to begin my summary conclusions with "In short" or "In conclusion."

5

Four Pillars of Personal Branding Success: A Brand Building Model to Position Your Brand

Follow your bliss and doors will open where there were no doors before.

—*Joseph Campbell*

These four pillars of personal branding success outline practical steps for you to incorporate in building your cohesive in-person and online platform to support your brand building efforts.

- Pillar 1: Create Your Personal Branding Profile
- Pillar 2: Identifying Your Unique Brand Promise, Target Market, Personal Branding Statement, and Personal Positioning Statement
- Pillar 3: Communicate Your Brand's Story with "On-Purpose" Messages
- Pillar 4: Connect and Grow Your Network

The exercises you will complete in pillars 1 and 2 will guide you in establishing personal branding documents that express the sum of the elements you've identified as making your brand both valuable and distinctive to your target. Once you've established your personal branding profile, allow it to serve as your accountability partner in remaining in line with how you identify with yourself, the promise you're committing to your market, and your goals. In embodying your personal brand offerings, share your story as a means to become an influencer to those who seek information, services, or products.

Now your goal is to educate others around who you are by sharing information about industry trends, thought leaders affecting your space, and organizations and events that are shaping the social, cultural, and academic climate of your industry and interests. As more people become exposed to your brand, make sure they leave the interaction knowing your name and something of which you're proud. You're going to package your visual identity with high-resolution images, professional promotional materials, and a strong off- and online presence. Your brand can't (and shouldn't) try to appeal to everyone. You'll never be able to communicate all facets of yourself with your target. So pillars 1 and 2 will lead you to shape your brand story composed of those carefully thought-out offerings you've identified in Chapter 3. Your unique story will resonate with the people who find value in what you represent. That connection will become the driving force behind their decision to return to your social platforms, invite you to events, hire you, collaborate with you, and keep the lines of communication with you open.

Unless your goal is becoming a knock-off brand of someone else, remain focused on your sacred seed of authenticity. Otherwise, it'll appear you're masquerading as someone you're not. To avoid this, these pillars will guide you through communicating your own brilliant story with authenticity, confidence, and consistency.

Personal Branding Success Pillar #1: Create Your Personal Brand Profile (Comprise of Your Needs, Core Values, Capabilities, Personal Brand Attributes, Passion, Mission, Vision and Goals)
Your personal brand profile defines the aggregation of elements you have identified about yourself and what you know about your target market. It mixes the various components of your personal brand to help you see a clear picture of the full scope of who you are.

Your brand story is more than a plot you create to share with people. It's bigger than what you say, your collateral materials, the words on your website, and your social media activity. It's a culmination of what you believe are the most salient experiences shaping your identity and supporting you in serving others. It's your overarching authentic expression: the main idea of your life, composed of character traits, know-hows, experiences, and preferences. Everything you present—your persona, the packaging of your marketing materials, the initiatives you support, and the way you spend your time—makes up that story. Intend to have every aspect of it mirror the truth of who you are to yourself first and second, to your target market.

Become knowledgeable of those you've committed to serving with your gift: your talents, skills, passion, and energy. Purposely understand their goals and needs and pledge to provide exceptional service to fill those needs. As humans, we're extremely complex, multidimensional beings, but the discipline of branding forces us to center our tactical efforts around delivering on our brand promise to our target market.

By its very nature of communicating points of differentiation, brand building is most successful when the person, product, or service being branded specializes in a distinct area of expertise. Your differentiating points provide you solid ground to establish the benefits and points of uniqueness of both your rational (capabilities) and emotional (character) value. In meeting new people, be prepared to communicate briefly but specifically about what you do best. What are the capabilities you possess that others don't? What know-hows have you developed better than most? What segments or subsegments of the population do you enjoy working with, or are naturally drawn to?

Allow your special combination of education, work experience, personal attributes, talents, and things you're passionate about to define your personal brand's niche. If you're a young professional enhancing your niche, you may feel unsure of the direction you want to take your talents. Most young professionals haven't focused much on embodying their uniqueness or understanding the full scope of their capabilities, and that's absolutely normal. While it's natural to get good at a lot of things throughout the course of your career your brand is packaged around what makes you unique and intriguing.

BEGIN CREATING YOUR PERSONAL BRAND PROFILE

Your personal brand profile should clearly spell out the person you perceive yourself to be, who you're talking to, and why. It should help you see the full scope of your brand, so take ownership and pride in crafting it.

Become synonymous with your brand promise; live and breathe the unique promise of value that your personal brand brings to those you serve.

In your personal branding journal in the back, begin crafting your personal brand profile by bringing together each of the below elements (covered in Chapter 3) of your brand as outlined below. (Refer to your journal notes from chapter 3):

Needs: Your immediate needs (making enough money to pay your bills, moving to a different city, landing a job in your field, switching your career path, reinventing yourself, starting a business, landing new clients, or fulfilling the sacred mark of your heart to pursue your dreams).

Core Values: Leading the emotional charge of your life, those principles that provide meaning for you. Core values are the set of standards that determine your choices, preferences, attitudes, and actions.

Capabilities: Gives you competence or proficiency to do something. Your education, work experience, skills, and strengths are all capabilities you've garnered. Use them as reinforcement in making yourself feel confident in your offerings. Capabilities are those skills others benefit from through working or connecting with you—providing security if you're a police officer, being a leader if you're a manager, the price point of your service if you're a consultant, or how quickly a client can get on your calendar for service if you're a service provider.

Personal brand attributes: What emotional senses do people feel when they hear your name? People want to connect with, work with, and associate with people they trust are competent, but they must be able to relate to them. Your emotional value is the intrinsic appeal you have that connects you emotionally with others. When applying for a new job or in seeking a new client (assuming you can provide the benefits the opportunity calls for), your emotional value often differentiates you from the competition.

Passions: Things that intrigue, excite, or inspire you. Your passions should dictate how you spend your spare time. Which activities do you love to the point that you could engage with them for hours at a time?

IDENTIFYING YOUR PERSONAL MISSION AND VISION STATEMENTS

Now that you've recorded the elements of your sacred seed of authenticity to compose the basis of your personal brand profile it's time to identify your personal mission and vision statements to add to your profile.

Mission statement: Your mission statement is used to simplify your purpose and communicate the mark you want to create in the world. It embodies your purpose and philosophy, and it should be used to drive your behaviors in supporting your best self. Consider it the sentence or two that sums up the essence of your brand. Prior to deciding on your mission statement, think about your core values, passions, and motives. Utilize your brand attributes as keywords to compile a mission that fully embraces who you are and expresses the driving force behind '*why*' you're driven to do the things you do.

In the same notion that a brand's logo or a state flag symbolizes the core of what's important for it, your personal mission reflects what's meaningful for you.

Consider these tips before crafting your mission statement:

- Begin with two of your personal brand attributes, the words you feel best describe how you are perceived or how you want to be perceived in the world.
- Think of the rational values that describe you; consider nouns that define what you do. Are you or do you want to be a strategist, educator, connector, or provider?
- Imagine the influence or impact you'd like to see in the world. What mark do you hope to contribute to the world?
- Have it capture your big "why." Why do you do the things you do?

MY MISSION IS AS FOLLOWS:

To live a happy life, serve those I'm passionate about, and make a positive mark in the world.

Vision: Your vision is the ideal version of how you'll live out your mission. It should clarify the brand offerings you want to lead with to achieve your goals. Consider it the guide to keep all your branding activities on purpose. Your vision is what you aspire to achieve long term. It states how your mission will look once it has been done.

Have your vision express your core values and what you're passionate about, especially the fundamental values that inspire you to achieve the brand promise on which you're building your reputation.

Contemplate the following in preparing your vision:

- Challenge the power of your words to paint a vivid picture of what it would be like to achieve your goal.
- Own it. Write it in the present tense to reflect now and the future.
- Your vision is bigger than your own personal contributions; it's inclusive of your role in achieving a larger picture.
- It should be clear, powerful, compelling, and meaningful to you. It's your plan to close the gap between where you are and where you're headed.
- Visualize the best version of yourself. Get a clear picture. What value are you contributing in the world? How are you making that contribution?
- If you had a magic wand and could do anything in the world, what would that thing be? What would you do once you were granted that thing? Why is that thing so important to you? Who or what does that thing serve and why?

MY VISION IS AS FOLLOWS:

I share the insight and proficiencies I've honed in brand marketing fused with my life's experiences to help others package, position, and leverage their brand stories. I love strategizing innovative and meaningful ways to help others service those most valuable to them. I feel happy helping myself, my loves, and socially conscious brands prosper.

Brand goals: What are the things you want to achieve: short (one to two years), medium (three to five years), and long term (more than five years)?

Head back to your personal branding journal in the back and add your mission and vision statements to your personal brand profile.

Personal Branding Success Pillar #2: Identifying Your Unique Brand Promise, Target Market, Personal Brand Statement, and Personal Positioning Statement

Your personal brand has to offer a brand promise that delivers a unique value to your target market: your audience, consumers, employer, potential employer, or clients. The unique promise of value you provide should serve as an important benefit to your target. It'll be used to establish your value currency with them, as they'll depend on you to deliver on that promise over and over again.

Communicating to your target in meaningful ways will position you as a respectable contributor around the topics you choose to highlight. The consistency in what you say and the behaviors you engage in should reinforce the story you're telling and bind the connective tissue between you and them. Once you take the time to understand the emotional triggers of your target and what motivates them, commit yourself to communicate to them messages you believe will resonate the most with them. Use the intrinsic values your brand attributes possess as the emotional exchange linking your brand to their needs.

Once you're clear on your unique promise of value and the target market you're seeking to share that promise with, you can begin putting together your personal brand and personal positioning statement. Your personal brand statement expresses what you represent, and should be used to lead you in making good "on-brand" or, for the sake of this guide "on-purpose" decisions that support activities leading you toward your goals.

BRAND PROMISE

Your brand promise identifies what you've committed to build your brand's reputation upon. Therefore, choose a brand promise you can repeatedly live up to.

Here's what Emily Davis, the aspiring junior public relations professional who also makes and sells jewelry, could use as her unique brand promise:

"I have an entrepreneurial spirit. I'm assertive, creative, and self-motivated. I'm an exceptional communicator and value myself as a team player. I diligently complete every creative project I work on, interjecting passion from start to finish. For each initiative, I get clear directives, a goal, and a corresponding timeline. I'm an avid photographer and use my creative eye to take captivating images to enhance my social-media responsibilities for the organizations I work with. My leaders and peers appreciate my knowledge of and passion for creating artistic, conversation-starting communication messages."

TARGET MARKET/AUDIENCE

Your target market or audience can consist of your future employer; an organization you want to do business with; clients or other people with similar ideals or interests as you; and colleagues, industry influencers, and leaders. It's the group or audience of people you've identified that you want to serve using your brilliance. Most times they'll share interests, passions, or desires with you. Those similarities may be geographic, industrial, socioeconomic, cultural, or psychographic; or mission, goal, or lifestyle driven.

You may not know specifically whom you serve or want to serve. Still, it's important to figure it out. Once you hone in on your target, fully educate yourself on what they need. Do they want information, entertainment, or inspiration? Given your offerings, contemplate how you can make the biggest impact in serving those needs. You want your target to feel confident you're capable of doing what you say you're going to do. So you'll need to work toward building credibility with them. Make sure your actions support the person you say you are and do what you say you'll do. In repeatedly delivering your brand promise to your target, your brand will build credibility. Once you establish integrity with your target, ask them for references, quotes, or testimonials to use in the future.

PERSONAL BRAND STATEMENT

Consider the overall themes that emerged from your personal brand profile and begin to envision your ideal self. Your personal brand statement is a paragraph that expresses that ideal self. As you start compiling your statement consider using words that feel empowering in describing what you have to offer the world. Use words that inspire and evoke positive emotions from you.

POSITIONING STATEMENT

Your positioning statement helps you illustrate how to position yourself to your market. It educates your target on elements that differentiates you from your competitors. It's the blueprint for your brand's identity, the compass that guides all your communication messages. It should culminate with the insight you've learned about your target, and direct you in positioning yourself to them. Allow your positioning statement to become the framework for delivering your promise and the benefits you're offering. With that, consider positioning yourself in a way that offers your market an opportunity. Can you solve a problem for them? Which particular need can you meet? Remember, the leverage in great positioning comes from placing yourself in the shoes of the market you aim to serve. This helps you better understand how to authentically fill their desires with the aptitudes you have. Once you spend time getting to understand the mind-set, unmet needs, and desires of your target- this can go a long way in helping you service them.

Use this opportunity to craft your brand's communication messages in a voice authentic to you that speaks to those needs and wants. Your target benefits from knowing what value you can provide to make their lives better.

Consider Emily Davis from Chicago who seeks to land a job as a junior public relations coordinator in arts or fashion.

Here is a snapshot of Emily's goals, target market, and competitive differences, the information she'll need to write her positioning statement:

Short-Term Goal: I seek to obtain an entry- or junior-level position in public relations in the arts or fashion industry.

Long-Term (Three-Year) Goal: My long-term goal is to become a public-relations manager for a company in the arts or fashion industry.

Define Your Target Market (Who You Want to Serve): My target market consists of art or fashion organizations, corporations, or institutions in Chicago, New York, or San Francisco with an in-house public relations department.

Target Market's Need or Problem: My target market needs a junior-level public relations coordinator who is creative, meticulous, and understands social media best practices.

Industry: I am a communications graduate with an emphasis on public relations that volunteers as a teacher of art at Art Chicago; also manages its social media platforms.

Competitive Differentiation: Unlike some recent public relations graduates, I have taken on a leadership role with an organization in my industry, gaining experience in social media and events planning. I was a student member of Public Relations Society of America and garnered leadership experience as vice president for my college chapter for two semesters.

Personal Brand Statement: I'm energized by my connection to others and my belief that people want to connect. I love bringing that ideal into creating communication messages I know will evoke conversations around artistic expression.

Positioning Statement: For art and fashion organizations looking to expand their public relations department, I'm an assertive, creative, and self-motivated public relations graduate from DePaul University. I've acquired leadership skills serving as vice president for DePaul's PRSA collegiate chapter and now spend my weekends utilizing those skills teaching art to students and growing the social media accounts for Art Chicago. In three months, I have increased enrollment for my classes by

12 percent, while increasing the organization's following and social sharing by more than 10 percent.

Head to your journal in the back and jot down your brand promise and personal brand positioning statement. Prioritize your own immediate goals, your target needs, your brand category, competitive differentiation, and value proposition.

YOUR PERSONAL BRAND STATEMENT

In corporate branding, businesses have mission and vision statements that guide the corporate culture and communications of the organization. In building your personal brand, the same principles are helpful. Your personal brand statement is the part of your brand's profile charged with guiding the vision for your brand. Your unique promise of value and personal brand statement are partners, in that your statement should articulate your promise. Both should focus on what your target audience can expect from you and create the expectation of what you must always deliver. There's no one more qualified than you in determining how you want your life to play out. Although you can't control every aspect of your career, business, or brand's success, a cohesive personal brand statement puts your vision at the center of your focus.

Remember your personal brand statement represents the depth of you and reminds yourself of your own motivations. It synthesizes your qualities into a statement that will serve as the foundation to communicate your brand's story.

Personal Brand Statement: I interject strategy, creativity, and connectivity into the lives of professionals using my expertise in communications, marketing, and advertising with a professional, personalized, "on-purpose" approach.

Personal Branding Success Pillar #3: Communicate Your Brand's Story with "On-Purpose" Messages

The third personal branding success pillar is the art of communicating your personal brand story: deciphering, messaging, and sharing your individual script to those you serve. As the CEO, captain, and author of your brand, you're responsible for directing the communications you're comfortable sharing about your life's journey. Consider packaging the most prevalent experiences that led you to where you currently stand, woven by the brilliance you've accumulated along the way. How should you do that? You know your life story better than anyone else! Share it your way, from your viewpoint, using your voice and persona to communicate with the people you want to serve.

If you're unclear around exactly what "on-brand" (or for the sake of this guide and your life, "on-purpose") means, think about Disney. The Disney brand sells magic. Anything about Disney relating to magic is "on-brand" or "on purpose"; things with no connection to magic are off brand and not marketed purposely. From time to time, there are moments and experiences at Disney that are less than magical. But we don't see those; it's not Disney's intent to allow consumers to engage with moments not aligned with the Disney brand story. Therefore, Disney's brand story won't publicly message, promote, or share those experiences. Everything Disney produces—movies, games, merchandise, travel, hospitality, music, and videos—is always messaging and demonstrating a story of magical ambiance. If the magic is readily identifiable, the concept is on-brand and purposeful; if not, it isn't.

Your story has immeasurable power to personify the way you identify with yourself, the causes you care about, and your purpose in the world. Your brand messages should succinctly communicate that story by educating your market about your viewpoints, insight, and experience. Together those messages, along with your supporting behavior and your visual identity, all shape the opinion your target and others form about you. Your messaging can be told through a myriad of ways: blog posts, speaking engagements, networking, volunteering, social media engagement, and word of mouth. Good old word of mouth is still a great way to have your brand story communicated to others.

In crafting your story, consider sharing those experiences that have had the biggest impact in determining your capabilities, ideals, personal interests, passions, and affiliations. Your brand is competing against everything in existence for mind share in the thoughts of those you're aiming to serve. As valuable as what you have to offer may be,

Americans are inundated on a daily basis by paid media (advertising), earned media (press coverage), and social media. Everything is competing with everything else in existence for a piece of attention and influence. In advertising, marketing messages work by building frequency to make impressions. The same reigns true in personal branding. It's natural for most people not to notice (much less appreciate) your brand only after receiving a few impressions or exposures. So the more you get your brand in front of the people you want to educate about who you are and what you're offering, the more memory and impact your brand will make.

Have fun and experiment with your messaging. Aim to have them connect with your target in thought-provoking, emotionally appealing, and relevant ways. Everything you communicate in branding shapes your story: so your biography, your social media platforms, your blog or website, your résumé, and your elevator pitch should all tell an intriguing but consistent story about you. A story composed of the things you want to communicate about yourself in public (off-/online and verbally/nonverbally) that will form the imprint people's minds will receive and process about you.

Keep your brand promise and positioning statement at the forefront of how you share your story. Consider politicians: they're great storytellers who have learned to use their stories, experience, and presence to galvanize their constituents and inspire others to follow them. Impactful storytellers influence their audiences by evoking emotions around their unmet needs, fears, or desires. They engage them to act upon something. Across all countries, cultures, and classes, stories are the universal language that connects people. Intriguing storytelling begins with an interesting story to share. Aim to communicate effectively the things within your offerings your target wants, believes, aspires to become, or yearns to know more about. Although it's your account to tell your story in your own voice, it's ultimately up to the audience to decide if it's relevant to them.

You will resonate, build trust, and achieve the goals you want with some people, while not being of interest at all to others. That's to be expected. Coca-Cola is one of the most recognizable brands in the world, and although the brand has billions of consumers, there are people who don't drink dark soda and will never have a Coke. Consequently, if you remove the label, it becomes just another cola, reflecting the established value The Coca-Cola Company has built around its beverage. Not everyone will resonate with, trust, or even like your brand. Diversity, preferences, and differences in opinions, values, personalities, and overall value currency make personal branding so darn cool. Set out to genuinely convey who you are, and the people you resonate with will become your ideal target. Never take your branding efforts personally. Find your validation through having the courage to put your story, your yearning to do more in the world, and your collective brilliance on blast; don't just expect everyone to perceive it positively. Really, that's not your business.

So, what is your business? Understanding, positioning, and sharing the power of your unique collection of values, experiences, and perceptions with the people having an interest or need to connect or collaborate with you. Once you decide which messages you want to share, craft a great elevator pitch, biography, and social media messages in ways that highlight your account. Center your messaging from authentic expressions of your life experiences, loves, pet peeves, behaviors, beliefs, and dreams.

By being your authentic self and communicating those messages, you'll attract the people and causes you're meant to serve. They'll show up in the capacity they're meant to.

BRAND MESSAGE

Authentic personal branding centers around messaging the story behind the whole person, with points of individuality greater than your professional experiences; it harnesses both your rational and emotional values. For instance, those brands that position themselves as premium or high-end traditionally explore luxury, access, convenience, or exclusivity as value propositions. Hence, those brands must aim to communicate their message to a segment of the market that prefers premium products, services/people to service them and are willing to pay higher prices to receive the benefits of a perceived higher caliber of service, luxury benefits, and access to things they wouldn't have admittance to otherwise. The same principle holds true for elite professional service providers, for example consultants. If you're a high-end marketing consultant, you may expect to share messages and communicate your brand's story highlighting fancy client lunches or dinners, VIP tickets to high-demand sporting, music, or theatrical events, and access to your own high-end network.

WRITING YOUR BIOGRAPHY

An important part of your story is your biography. A snapshot of your career and personal history woven with a sense of your character. Your biography should tell a story that leaves the reader feeling intrigued and curious to know more about you. You can't be all things to all people, so choose points to highlight that are important to you.

Contemplate implementing these tips when writing or refreshing your bio:

- Write in the third person and from an objective point of view. (Third person makes your writing appear journalistic.)
- Start with a strong opening paragraph.
- Share your brand promise.
- Include your brand value.
- Keep it positive and upbeat.
- Stay away from clichés.
- Keep it to one page for every ten years.

Consider sharing the following personal insights:

- Your personal brand statement
- Measurable achievements ("I increased sales by 30 percent")
- Your personal interests (such as sports or musical instruments played, or "I went to 4-H camp religiously and rode dirt bikes")
- Work, volunteer, and leadership experience
- Your education and certifications

77

- Life experiences that were significant in shaping you
- Life lessons

People are inquisitive about one another. We enjoy learning about each other's stories. Use your biography to let others into your world. It's an appropriate opportunity to pat your own back for the things you've achieved and learned, while giving the reader a sense of your personality.

Then there is your elevator pitch. Think of your elevator pitch as your own commercial. It should be shorter than your biography and explain what you do along with supporting evidence and value. It's a great idea to have two pitches you can roll with at any time, a shorter and a longer version.

Emily's shorter pitch would go something like this:

Thirty-Second Elevator Pitch: "I'm Emily Davis, a 2016 public relations graduate from DePaul University. On weekends, I enjoy teaching art education at Art Chicago, where I've strategically grown the Twitter, Facebook, and Instagram accounts by 22 percent in three months. Social media engagement continues to be increasingly important to the future of public relations, and I'm committed to staying on top of the industry's best practices."

SIXTY-SECOND ELEVATOR PITCH

Although an introduction could go from ten seconds to a few minutes, the key remains becoming confident in speaking about yourself. Your sixty-second elevator pitch is the equivalent of a corporate brand's sixty-second advertising commercial. Let it become your on-deck script to introduce yourself. Begin by stating who you are and what you do. Then incorporate a few distinct elements of your brand.

Craft an elevator pitch you feel will pique the interest of others. It'll serve as one of the most common tools you'll use in building your personal brand. It's both ideal and convenient for networking; the more comfortable you become speaking about yourself, the stronger impact you'll make. People are similar at our core. We're all drawn to those people, places, and things that interest us and spark our curiosity. In the beginning, your elevator pitch may not feel natural. If that's true for you, you've probably thought about it too much. However, the more comfortable you become stating who you are and what's important to you, the more connections you'll have.

It's helpful to incorporate these tips when introducing yourself:

- Always know as much as you can about those you'll be speaking to.
- Always lead with your name and one other thing you're proud of. "Hi, I'm Emily, a recent communications graduate from DePaul University."
- Keep your personal brand and the brand promise that you bring to your audience at the top of your mind.
- Show enthusiasm about who you are and what you do.
- Don't be too personal. Sharing that your best friend is waiting for you in the car because you didn't have the money to pay for parking is too much information.
- Be confident. There is no one in the world better at being you than you. Even if you're not confident, take a deep breath, listen up, and go with the flow.
- Stand tall, keep your shoulders pushed back, and maintain strong eye contact. Show a strong sense of presence.
- Never discuss controversial, debatable, or difficult subjects. When you don't know enough about the other person's perspective, err on the safe side.
- Keep it short. Introduce yourself, have small talk, exchange contact information, and move on.
- Don't give your whole résumé or life history. Avoid overwhelming people by telling them too much too soon. Remember that you want to keep them interested and curious. If you tell them everything, there's nothing left to be curious about.
- Listen more and speak less. People love to feel like you're interested in them. Once you say who you are, genuinely engage them by finding out more about them.

- Don't share personal or inappropriate information about other people. Keep it positive and light. Unless your teeth are missing because you just came from the dentist, don't share that.
- Don't always rely on your rehearsed elevator pitch. Go with the natural flow of the conversation. Size up your listener and free flow as necessary.
- Practice in front of a mirror, over and over, until you feel comfortable with different variations of your pitch.

Emily's Sixty-Second Elevator Pitch: "I'm Emily Davis, a recent public relations graduate from DePaul University. During my senior year, I served as vice president of my campus chapter of the Public Relations Society of America. On weekends, I enjoy teaching art education while managing the Twitter, Facebook, and Instagram accounts for Art Chicago. Social media continues to be increasingly important to future of public relations, and Art Chicago trusts me to handle their accounts."

Personally, I use my blog (www.TheBrandistaGuide.com) and personal website (www.CourtneyRRhodes.com) as the foundation for creating content and sharing my story with my audience. I support those messages and stories using social media, speaking engagements, and networking opportunities. For me, it works like this: I have an editorial calendar that lists the content I'm posting for the week. From my posts, I highlight important tidbits to share on my social platforms that connect back to the post.

Identify your core messages and spend the majority of your posting and communications around them. I communicate my brand story by keeping my core messages or content themes about things related to entrepreneurship, personal branding, marketing, women's empowerment, and professional development. Identify your key messages and consistently deliver your personalized message regarding them across the communication channels that work best for you. The communication channels you choose will become your means to build brand awareness both on- and offline. Discover the best mix of mediums (based on who you're trying to reach) most effective to share your message, and continue to reevaluate the success of your mix.

CONTENT THEMES

Content themes are composed of key phrases or keywords, causes you support, interests and areas of specialty you have, and other content necessary to communicate the full spectrum of your brand's story. Your content themes are the topics you identify to best message things of interest in your life you're willing to highlight via your communication channels. Stick to themes around the subjects you're interested in, and you'll become a go-to source for people.

Defining content themes will help you serve the needs, wants, and desires of the market you're aiming to influence. To do this, interject the best of your personality and brand attributes into the mix of information and content you've chosen to become the go-to brand for. That big, brilliant personality of yours is charged with bringing resonance by making your messages personal and leaving your target feeling like you're directly speaking to them. Consider your perspective regarding the topic you're sharing and add personal commentary. Share experiences that have led you to the position you hold today. You're the curator of your brand's story, and your unique perspective, voice, and content themes are what people will be drawn toward.

Identify those subjects in which you're well versed and have a genuine interest, and then write or share content around those topics. Use strong visuals, including photographs and videos, to best capture what you're intending to portray. Remember to interject your character. Are you humorous? Strategic? Charismatic? Embrace those brand attributes to accentuate the voice you communicate through. Content buckets and keywords or hashtags are great branding tools, so select three to six strong hashtags for each bucket.

CAREER BUCKET

Your career bucket is where you'll discuss content relating to your career and industry. Consider topics relating to job opportunities, professionals on the move, thought leaders, trends, innovations, conferences, seminars, networking events, and continuing-education opportunities. Choose subjects that allow you to highlight your rational value, professional capabilities, what's happening in and around your career, and professional expertise.

PASSION BUCKET

Your passion bucket is where you get to express the best of the things you love. Consider it your outlet to create, comment, or share content around those personal experiences, social or political causes, or activities you're passionate about. This content can revolve around your family life, hobbies, a side hustle you have, a class you're taking, a hobby you're embracing, an evening out, a cause you're supporting, or anything that intrigues you. Take advantage of those opportunities that permit you to showcase your emotional values and individuality.

COMMUNICATION STRATEGY

Creating a strategy to direct your communication plan is beneficial to keep your brand's message on purpose in adhering to the content themes you've chosen to communicate your brand story. Remain focused on the goal you're attempting to accomplish in communicating to your target and the most viable communication channels to reach them. If no one in your industry knows you yet, your goal should be to become more visible and pique the interest of your industry's clients, students, hiring managers, recruiters, influencers, and others you've targeted.

The majority of your messages should be on purpose to your own goals; align with how you've decided to brand yourself; and reinforce your brand's promise of value. Your style, persona, the words you use, the causes you support, and the visual identity you use in your communication messages shape the impressions that largely influence the minds of others.

If you're Emily Davis branding yourself as the confident and charismatic junior public relations executive who specializes in fashion and the arts, deliver communication messages (visually and verbally) that show you confidently engaging in those things. Forget about insecure, obsessive moments of binge eating in bed and crying over your latest breakup. That's not a part of your brand's story. More importantly, it opposes your on-purpose behavior as a confident, charismatic public-relations professional. That one image could tarnish your reputation by sending a contradictory message. Remember, perception is reality in the world of branding. Impressions are lasting and unfortunately not very forgiving. Since it's not the direction you've chosen to move toward with your brand, save the non-supporting visuals for girls' night in, when you're in the company of your friends in a judgment-free safe zone with nothing on the line.

Everyone has vulnerable moments, and those are often our biggest opportunities for growth; however, in the discipline of branding there is a gray area between *vulnerability* and *immaturity*. The latter doesn't serve your branding goals or support the value you're working to establish with your target.

COMMUNICATIONS PLAN

Creating, implementing, and committing your personal brand's communications (marketing plan), will keep you from disappearing for weeks or months, more than enough time for people to forget about you. I'm all for personal brands creating personal blogs, websites, newsletters, being aggressive at attending events, and networking to become and remain visible. You'll only be relevant when other people are aware of what you're offering. No matter how amazingly brilliant you become at mastering your expertise, if no one knows about your brilliance, how much influence can it have? Communicate your story through everything from your actions to your written communications to your body language and style. After identifying the communication tools and channels to most effectively speak to your target, commit to regularly engaging with them. Based on the amount of time you're willing to spend on your personal branding efforts, dedicate a specific period of time daily or weekly to create content for yourself. Update and engage your digital presence weekly, if not daily (depending on your goals) to keep your target audience engaged. Again, the amount of time you spend on your social channels is up to you, but if it's an important part of the communication mix, do it often and well.

Hashtags are a great way to build brand resonance digitally on social media and elsewhere online. Identify, at minimum, four (but no more than ten) hashtags to use across Twitter, Instagram, Google+, and Facebook. Give yourself a nice balance of career and personal tags. If your brand highlights more of your personal life, dedicate the majority of your hashtags to your personal life. If the majority of your communication messages or posts are career or success driven, use corresponding hashtags. The balance between career and professional tags should correlate with your own brand and the goals you have for branding. Emily, the recent public relations graduate who loves supporting the local art club and lives in Chicago, could use #ArtMatters, #ArtChicago, or #ArtPRGirl. Have fun with hashtags, be interesting, but remember, consistency is key in building online communities.

Head to your personal branding journal, draft your biography and the copy for three social media posts from your passion bucket. An example of Emily's post would be as follows:

Instagram, Twitter, Pinterest, or Facebook: Post a picture from Chicago's Art in the Park event with the copy: "Still on cloud nine from an overload of talented artists, art students, and Chicago art lovers I connected with at Art in the Park. #ArtChicago #ArtPRGirl #ChicagoConnects"

Why not take it a step further and schedule your communications plan for the week? Pick a day each week to think through what content you have over the next few days, and schedule your postings on your calendar as you would other appointments.

Ideas on how to gather and share your brand's content:

- Join and become active with professional organizations.
- Volunteer with a cause and community-development projects.
- Create a blog.
- Contribute to someone else's blog or newsletter.
- Attend networking events.
- Speak at events, company outings, or any opportunity you have.
- Create your profile on social-media sites.

- Join social-media groups for career professionals.
- Join LinkedIn groups and engage in them.
- Comment on other people's blogs and corporate sites.

In maximizing your brand's communication, consider utilizing the following branding activities:

- Brand your e-mail signature.
- Create an electronic press kit or a one-sheet around you, your niche, job, business, or services, and your signature speaking topics.
- Create a blog for your area of expertise or passion.
- Write a monthly newsletter for your industry. You can either have at it solo or include contributors.
- Plan a signature event and invite experts in your industry to share valuable insight and industry trends. You can make it as informal or high-end as you want it, but align it with your own personal brand.
- Comment on industry blogs and link back to your website or blog.
- Write articles based on your niche or area of specialty and post them online.
- Continue to hone your level of expertise by pursuing continuing education through classes, workshops, seminars, and coaching opportunities. The more you know, the more sustainable you'll be.

Personal Branding Success Pillar #4: Connect and Grow Your Network
In building your brand you're charged with connecting in communities and networks of people to share resources, promote common interests, and build awareness around what you offer. As you build your network, the connections you make play an important role toward the influence you'll garner and the visibility you'll have.

When people ask you to tell them about yourself, be prepared to speak in a way that's easy to comprehend. Keep your language simple and to the point. Consider an introduction that leads with a short summary of your background as a means to establish some credibility upfront. When possible include something the two of you have in common, whether it's a person, interest, or prior experience. As you share information about who you are, it establishes a foundation to build trust and competency around later. Trust remains the foundation for good relationships, and competency solidifies them. After sharing your short introduction, if he or she hasn't done so, ask your listener to share his or her background with you. Listen with the intent to do nothing other than absorb the information. Be mindful not to lose the moment by anticipating what to say next, stay in it and allow the conversation to follow its natural flow.

Practice repeating out loud and getting comfortable with the answer to "Tell me about yourself." Your response will establish the foundation for your new relationship and the potential of moving beyond the introduction. It promptly reveals what you feel is valuable about yourself and what's important to you.

When answering, "Tell me about yourself," you're disclosing and indicating the following:

- How confident you are in yourself and your capabilities, a traditional indicator about your future successes
- How you feel regarding your own background, accomplishments, and what's possible for your life
- How good you are at communicating your thoughts
- Your energetic vibes

In a networking setting, often the people you're connecting with won't have enough time to get to know you. What they're doing is getting to know your personal brand: who you are, what you do, and for whom you do it. As you add new people to your contacts, remember to reinforce and nurture the professional relationships you already have. For young professionals, consider solidifying relationships with college professors, internship coordinators, supervisors, and leaders from organizations you were involved with. Nurture and strengthen those relationships. For business owners, influencers, and career professionals, consider organizational affiliations, industry clubs, and current clients or colleagues and their affiliated networks to extend your network.

Consider sending your current connections birthday and holiday cards or a note to say you're thinking of them. For the new ones, drop them a note to say you're looking forward to your newfound connection while reiterating something you learned about them during your initial introduction. The goal is to make a positive impression with them so they remember who you are. Networking is an excellent opportunity for you to broaden and extend your alliances. In major cities, there are an abundance of great professional networking events and mixers. Never allow complacency for your brand. In bringing awareness to your offerings, there will always be new, intriguing, and interesting people worth meeting. Check out as many networking events as you can, always put forth the best of your brand, and remember you're networking to build your professional connections. Get out, introduce yourself, talk to people, find out what they're doing, and make connections, connections, and more connections. In no time, you'll build your network by initiating dual relationships with those whose network you want to join.

In meeting new people, seek to get to know them personally and professionally. Share relevant information with them by connecting them with other networking opportunities, information, or people you believe would enhance their brands. There's an old saying that your network becomes your net worth; true or not, the more people you can positively connect and build trust with, the more people who will be talking about what you do and making introductions for you. Again, the key is advancing the connection as a give-and-take relationship. One-sided relationships tend not to last long. Your network is a direct extension of your brand, showing your target market/audience who already trusts *you*.

In the blink of an eye, your appearance, body language, how you communicate, and what you have to say will send imprints that can confirm or contradict your brand. Make it a priority for you to embrace "on-purpose" behaviors; they'll reinforce the brand you've decided to build. When you're confident and your personal brand is authentic, networking is a fabulous source for new relationships. Effectively done, networking leads to new opportunities, referrals, and beneficial two-sided relationships.

There are a myriad of ways a contact you meet through networking can benefit your brand:

- Become a mentor
- Become a valuable advisor
- Refer opportunities to you
- Hire you or become a client
- Offer expertise in different areas
- Introduce you to other people who could be beneficial to you
- Be a connector to influential people in your industry, the media, or politics

BUILDING AND ENGAGING YOUR MARKET THROUGH SOCIAL-MEDIA PLATFORMS

Surveys suggest LinkedIn's membership has reached approximately 58.5 million accounts in the United States, with an estimated working population of around 180 million. It's assumed that 32.5 percent of America's workforce owns a LinkedIn profile. Topping LinkedIn, about 50 percent of Americans have Facebook accounts, while 34 percent of the population engages on Twitter, and 20 percent of Internet users use Instagram. What does this mean for your brand? Several things: first, if you've made your information publicly available online, potential employers, contractors, and stalkers alike have access to your online personal profiles and current activity; second, you have unlimited access to connect with millions of people from behind your computer, iPad, or mobile device to direct your brand in ways that align with your goals.

The digital age makes branding and marketing easier, but it also makes tarnishing your brand easier than ever as well. The Internet gives you the ability to connect with your market twenty-four hours a day, seven days a week. In our wired existence, companies and individuals alike have access to cyber vetting, also known as online vetting, a technique frequently used to vet the Internet reputation and online presence of potential employees and contractors. There is easy access to everyone's digital footprint through open-source information, which accesses content publicly available through search engines and social media sites. As with your other communication channels, you must decide how much you'd like to connect on each of your social platforms as well as determine what types of messages and content you want to make available. If you're an entrepreneur, blogger, influencer, or consultant who brings in revenue from the Internet, provides online services, gets clients, or is actively building an online audience, take the time to map out your social media strategy.

For each of your social platforms, create an editorial calendar of how many days a week or times a day—depending on your industry, brand, or goals—you want to engage in your online communities. Use your editorial calendar to serve as your minimum social posting plan; then remain fluid to tweak it as relevant information becomes available or interesting content catches your attention. The market you want to offer your capabilities to and serve may connect with a multitude of other personal brands offering similar competencies on a regular basis. Focus your social media content on keeping your brand promise clear, your messaging and brand image consistent, and lead with as much on-purpose messaging as possible.

Social media allows you to direct impressions that are more personal than written communication tools. Your online presence has the support of aligning visual images or videos to help support what you've written.

Use your personal website or blog to serve as the online hub for your personal brand, where people can go to find out more about you. Then create a similar look and feel for your social media platforms.

Consider these social media platforms to support your website or blog:

LinkedIn: Centers around the business community and is the leading platform for business networking. Keep your LinkedIn networking and content sharing professional. Opt to share only professional articles, insight, and content relative to business.

Facebook: Is designed to share images, videos, articles, and links to tell your story in engaging ways. The platform allows you to showcase both the personal and professional aspects of your brand.

Twitter: Gives you the opportunity to send and receive messages up to 140 characters long. It's a great place to solidify your expertise by providing targeted content and build a following around what you have to say.

Instagram: Offers a visual platform comprised of pictures and videos to share your personal brand and activities with friends, family, and like-minded individuals.

Pinterest: Provides a great opportunity for you to tell stories and organize the things you like and are interested in. You can create boards and pin photographs that inspire you.

Manage your personal brand messaging by following these guidelines:

- Google yourself every month or so, to stay on top of information floating on the World Wide Web about you.
- Use your personal brand attributes in everything you create. All your spoken and written communication needs to connect back to your personal brand attributes.
- Highlight the same brand attributes and perspective throughout your marketing documents.
- Steer away from activities and behaviors that don't positively support your brand.
- Speak and write about your capabilities, strengths, and brand attributes when communicating about the work you do.
- Choose consistent words and images to show synergy in your brand messaging.
- Communicate ideas and solutions that can be beneficial to your target market.

Every opportunity your brand has to get in front of potential consumers is called a touch point. Like corporate brands, you should remind your target market or audience at every touch point why they should hire, do business with, and connect with or support you. At any given time, they—or someone they know—could be looking to employ or hire someone with your capabilities, so you want them to consider your brand first. Before or as an organization is going through their recruitment or RFP process, you should be making positive impressions with them and subtly reminding them why you're the best candidate for the opportunity. Subsequently, once you secure the new position or piece of business, your behaviors should reiterate why they made the right decision in choosing you as an employee or partner.

Consider an automotive group in Atlanta, Georgia, that is looking to hire a branding or marketing consultant to create branded experiences for their consumers and potential consumers. The group's owner or management team would likely ask a trusted source for a referral. Their next step would be to do an online search for "brand-marketing consultants in Atlanta." If you're a brand-marketing consultant in Atlanta who recently made a Google+ post about a successful experience you created for a current client using the hashtag #BrandMarketingAtl, #BestOfAtlanta, or #CustomersMatter, there is a high probability your information will show up at the top of their organic search. No one has the exact formula for Internet algorithms, but I know it's one of consistency and accuracy. Therefore, the more" on-purpose" social-media posting and communicating online around your chosen keywords and hashtags, the more organically visible your brand will become on the Internet in the minds of those you want to attract.

YOUR BRAND IDENTITY

Your brand identity should involve a cohesive brand theme carried throughout all the branded items your target will see, touch, or experience. Your image, business card, stationery, and marketing materials should reflect the brand image your brand seeks to reflect. It's important to stay within what's acceptable for your particular profession's or industry's standards, while capturing your unique persona. If you're branding yourself as the charismatic, creative graphic artist who is a typography expert, touting a southern belle appeal, devise your branded promotional items to reflect that same essence. Everything that communicates something about you, from your website to social media backgrounds, will leave an imprint in the minds of others regarding your brand. If you have a website, have your similarly designed business card direct people to your website to learn more about you, your offerings, and your persona. Have fun and dare to create a distinct brand identity that aligns with your personality.

Consider having your business card showcase the following:

- Who you are
- What you do for a living
- Who you do it for
- How to connect with you on- and offline
- Visual appeal that represents your brand
- The visual brand-identity message you want to send about yourself
- Professionalism with high-quality paper and strong graphic design

Contemplate choosing a signature color and theme that'll stand out across all your business communications, promotional materials, and social media platforms. If you're an entrepreneur or influencer, work with a professional graphic artist or designer to create the theme for your collateral pieces. Make your visual-identity pieces consistent across all your branding touch points, making them identifiable for your market to associate everything supporting your brand as consistent with your look and feel.

SOCIAL MEDIA PROFILES AND BACKGROUND IMAGES
Your social media images and profile should match the brand identity of your other marketing communication tools. Use high-resolution, brand-appropriate images for all your profiles. When choosing a background image and profile picture, although it doesn't have to be identical to your other branded elements, it should have the same color theme and design aesthetic. Unless you're building a career as a promotional model for spirit brands, don't use party pictures as your backdrop.

Choose a strong, succinct elevator pitch about yourself from your biography and use snippets of it across your profiles. Invest the money to get professional, high-resolution images. If you have a smartphone, there are great apps for lighting, like Afterlight, VSCO, or Snapseed offering the capacity to make your images comparable to professional ones. Lighting, angles, and expressions matter in branding. Your images should represent the best of how you'd like to be portrayed. If you want to become a partner at a top accounting firm, project an image and behave like you're already a partner.

SOCIAL MEDIA ENGAGEMENT

Unfortunately, I hear stories of young people losing out on employment and career opportunities because a company performed a digital background check on them, only to perceive them as high risk. Yes, that's another very real component of the Internet: *everything* you share becomes public knowledge. We love that we can Google anything and gain access to an abundance of information on any subject. On the flip side, everything you've ever done digitally is on the World Wide Web, which can and will impact how your personal brand is being perceived.

For me, social media engagement sometimes equates to revenue, making it beneficial to my success. Yes, likes and shares translate into opportunities for consulting, brand partnerships, speaking opportunities, and other brand-influencer perks. Nonetheless, in the social media space, followers, shares, and likes aren't the ultimate measures for branding success. The engagement level of your target market or audience is more important to your branding than the overall numbers. Branding is a game of laser focus on your target and super service to the needs of those people. Branding is the godmother of the saying, "You can't be everything to everybody."

If your priority in personal branding is to establish yourself as a credible professional others will believe as competent and trustworthy, personal rants should never be on your social channels. First and foremost, it makes you appear emotionally unstable. Second, it's unprofessional. Third, it doesn't portray a good level of emotional intelligence.

Everything you do messages your story; make sure it's an intelligible representative of the perception you want others to process about your brand.

If you enjoy swaying toward shock value or the judgmental side of life, be prepared to stay in social media conflict. With goals for yourself and the sacred seed of your mark, a significant amount of your time on- and offline should be spent doing the work: providing service, networking, volunteering, developing your passions, and moving toward the life you're building. In committing to building your own brand and pursuing tangible goals, there's little time to negatively engage others on- or offline. Everything isn't for everybody. Spend your time and energies online connecting with others who align with your beliefs and the things you value. Good vibes attract more good vibes, just as powerfully as negativity fuels more negativity. Anything else is a waste of your time and will drain your energy. Give your attention to things that matter. Being judgmental is only beneficial if you've purposely chosen to build your brand around controversy and conflict.

It doesn't benefit you to have thousands of random followers if they don't engage with you. Ask yourself who is engaging with you on social media. Aim to attract followers in your target market, audience, or industry who are like-minded and can influence your career or goals. Branding is about quality over quantity, where content is king and engagement is queen. Trust me, a like or comment from @ DeeDaKilla is not the goal if he isn't in your market. Instead, have the objective of sharing content relevant to future employers, clients, people you inspire, community organizers for your interests or passion, and students coming behind in your field. Opt to share, tag, post, and comment on positive insight and information that'll prove helpful in engaging other like-minded individuals and the folks you're focused on reaching.

BUILD AND CONNECT WITH YOUR AUDIENCE AND NETWORK

As a purpose-driven brand, learning to build and connect with your audience to make the most of networking are ongoing processes. Strive to balance your time between building your online and offline networks. Why? Both in-person contacts and social-media followers can play an important role in your ability to build your overall brand awareness. It's not uncommon for digitally wired personal brands to have incredible brand ambassadors who share, support, and talk about everything they do. They are the modern-day word-of-mouth machine—on steroids.

Utilize these in-person networking opportunities and build connections:

- Don't make it a habit to eat lunch alone.
- Sit on panels or attend seminars and workshops about things you have an interest in.
- Join professional, athletic, and social cause organizations.
- Offer to serve on boards or committees.
- Host social and networking parties for your professional friends and connections.
- Find groups that attract your target market and attend their events.
- Attend and participate in charitable events that raise money for things you're passionate about.

When time allows, collaborate with for-cause organizations, community groups, and like-minded individuals to join forces on projects that align with your ideals and attributes.

Communicate your message with impact using the following communication best practices:

- Have something interesting to say and share it in your own voice. Use your personality and persona to bring your message to life.
- Engage in conversations on social media in your industry that are relevant to you or your market. If you have an opinion, express it. Comment, like, tweet, and share; just keep the conversation going.
- Follow industry thought leaders, influencers, and innovators on your social channels to stay informed.

- Stay pitch ready and know your elevator pitch; have a few versions of it you can share at any given time.
- Be a connector who brings people with common interests together.
- Once you connect with someone, say what you mean and mean what you say. Your connections will only be as valuable as the trust and competency you're able to build.

BE STRATEGIC IN PROMOTING YOUR BRAND

Let's talk strategy and execution. Exactly what is a personal branding strategy? Your personal branding strategy is equivalent to strategic marketing in corporate branding. It's a plan of action designed to give you tactical items to implement in order to achieve your branding goals. It creates longevity for your brand by taking your overarching branding goal and directing a communication plan that reflects who you are, what you do, and who you serve. Consider it your brand's game plan in moving from the self-reflection phase to the "Watch out world, here I am." stage.

Your personal brand strategy directs you to build greater awareness for yourself to achieve success, as represented by money, self-esteem, fulfillment, service, significance, or whatever measures are important to you. It's easier to follow through with your plan once you've identified detail activities you want to use to promote yourself. Remember that the key behind an effective personal brand strategy is consistency: consistent messages, consistent value, and consistent execution.

On top of respecting and enjoying what you do, it's helpful to continue learning and growing in your specialty, while refining your craft and building your reputation. Building anything requires an executable plan, actions, patience, and committed work.

You'll expand your brand awareness and educate more and more people about your brilliance by successfully completing the projects, jobs, engagements, and tasks you embark upon: one amazing social cause project completed, one inspiring speech delivered, one successful panel discussed, one blog post contribution, or one LinkedIn post at a time.

Become confident at pitching interesting projects, big achievements, or social movements to organizations that may have an interest in partnering with you. Share these insights and opportunities with journalists or influencers who may be willing to spread awareness about your project. When working on newsworthy endeavors, connections with people in the media, along with a strong press release, should become your best friends along the road to earning publicity. Whether pitching an event, book, promotion, seminar, fundraiser, or a career move to the media, influencers, and bloggers covering your industry, be prepared to discuss the who, what, when, where, and why of your news. Remember, the story doesn't have to be about you. Most times, it shouldn't be. It's more interesting when it's about something in which you're involved that's affecting the bigger picture of something relevant to the masses. Consider news around current events, relevancy for a particular season, relating to a trending topic or helpful to a particular cultural climate. Whether you're aiming to garner interest from a journalist, blogger, or organization to work with you, be creative when pitching your ideas, and lead with what's in it for the person or organization involved.

Keep these four pillars of personal branding success at the forefront of your brand building efforts and enjoy establishing your cohesive in-person and online branding platform.

6

Align Your Personal Image with Your Brand's Story

Whether you think you can, or you think you can't- you're right.

—Henry Ford

Your personal image is how you present yourself to the world. It's the culmination of how you style and groom yourself, the actions you take, what you say, how you say it, and your body language. As you journey through "on- purpose" living, your appearance should support you in sending the messages you've decided will best encourage your target market to have confidence in and trust you.

The manner in which you groom and style yourself, the verbal and nonverbal communications you express, and the way you behave in-person and online represent your personal image. From time to time, we've all been guilty of using words like *preppy, stylish, classy, hip, old-fashioned, elegant, fashion-forward, artsy, feminine, outdated, shabby-chic, grunge, punk,* or *interesting* to categorize someone's style. Whether we're aware of it or not, we place judgment on others based on their visual appearance and image. Your personal image is a prominent supporting element of your brand's identity and the emotional value that becomes synonymous with it.

We naturally create allegiances and loyalty to brands around the emotional expectations and preferences we've processed about them. The emotional value others place on your image will be as varied as their personal preferences. As a professional, you're charged with consistently working towards building trust and competency with your market through everything you do. Your image can either work to support or discredit your other brand messaging efforts. As one of your brand's limited tangible representations, as much as possible, take the opportunity to have your image reinforce your brand's story.

Walking into a room full of strangers, they'll form their first impression about you. Given they know nothing else about you, that impression will be solely based upon your appearance, body language, and personal vibe. Whether you enjoy putting your looks together or not, your image on- and offline is a part of your brand; in some instances, it'll determine the foundation for your connection with others. If the other person perceives your image as not professional enough, polished enough, confident enough, or self-aware enough (and the list goes on), they may choose not to further engage with you. In branding, corporate and personal, a person or product's image often gets the brand invited to "a seat at the table" or the possibility of being considered for a business opportunity or a sale. Your brand's capabilities and presentation at the table determines the direction the opportunity moves from there.

Perhaps you don't get excited about fashion, style, and self-expression; still, anyone committing the time to shape their brand should assure their appearance supports it. If you're packaging yourself as detail oriented when you don't exercise that level of care in presenting yourself, you risk discrediting your own story.

Reflect upon the six to eight personal brand attributes from Chapter 3 you chose to communicate your brand's story. Think of grooming and style choices that'll complement those attributes. Identical to the communication messages you send, the visual images you depict all send messages (sometimes subtle, other times not) to others. In turn, those messages contribute to influencing the views your audience will form about you. In making sure your personal image aligns with the brand you're crafting, keep your goals top of mind. If your plans include being CEO of an accounting firm, your personal image should reflect that of an aspiring CEO in the accounting industry. Consequently, if you dream of running a local tattoo parlor, you certainly have more flexibility to express your creative side. Your personal image should do two things: make you feel confident and powerful about how you're represented in the world and reinforce the mental imprints you want to send about your brand in the minds of others.

In her book, *Mind What You Wear: The Psychology of Fashion*, psychologist Karen J. Pine shares the result of research conducted while she worked as a professor at the University of Hertfordshire. For the project, Pine asked students to wear superhero clothing while spending time among their peers. She hypothesized that wearing the superhero gear would impact the thoughts and moods of the students wearing it. Not only did her theory prove to be true, but the students additionally reported an increase in confidence. They perceived themselves to be physically stronger, more likeable, and even superior to other students. Think about it, isn't looking fabulous the best serotonin rush? On those days you look great, your mood elevates, and you enjoy a pleasant boost of self-assurance. Therefore, for big meetings and important events, make it a priority to look (and accordingly, feel) your best.

DRESS FOR BRILLIANCE

If necessary, polish your image to authentically reflect the person you are or aspire to become. If you're a creative person, play with fun ways to convey that creative spirit. If you're destined to be a leader in a corporate setting, embrace those looks you feel best personify a person already in that position. Your personal style may likely continue to evolve as you do. However, there are small things you can do now to help support your cohesive visual identity.

As a career professional, your company's dress code may not allow you to be as expressive as you'd prefer, but when working for other people, you have to abide by their standards and corporate culture. You may be the most creative, expressive, and qualified creative director on the East Coast; however, if your image is just as expressive as your work, it may present challenges for you to land a job at one of the big advertising agencies. Although advertising agencies exist off creativity and strategy, in the workplace, advertising professionals have to adhere to the dress code of their company's culture. Educate yourself around the professional standards of the industry you're in, and more specifically, of the company or organization you're aiming to join or are a part of.

As a hiring manager, few things frustrated me more than meeting dynamic, qualified candidates I wanted to hire, only to get pushback from my superiors regarding their lack of confidence in the individual's ability to fit into the organization's corporate culture. In retrospect, the pushback was well meaning, but I'll never know if the candidates would've excelled or not. The corporation used a personality-profiling system to match the best-of-the-best current employee profiles to new candidates. I felt it was an innovative approach to match potential candidates with the company's standards. In hindsight, it didn't allow for much diversity. Here lies a major challenge and setback for many career professionals and their images.

Your style choices, hairstyle, and grooming regimen are reflections of how you express yourself. They play a vital part in how you're perceived. Although your visual image doesn't reflect your ability to do a particular job, it does direct mental marks others receive about you. This includes everything you embrace, from the colors, cuts, fabrics, and complexities of your outfits to your hair, makeup, grooming, and accessories. Whether you care or not, intend to brand yourself or not, or even care about how you're being perceived or not, we live in a world of impressions. From a branding standpoint, impressions make the brand go round. Still, the key remains knowing what you are and aren't flexible about. Ultimately you have no control over the foundation that built other people's psychoanalysis.

Unfortunately, there are too many bias stereotypes rearing their heads in the culture of corporate America. I find it unfair and downright closed-minded to know that in some organizations, wearing your hair neatly in its natural state could hinder you from career opportunities, but the reality is that it does. So in cultivating your on-purpose brand, recognize when and where those cultural biases exist, and decide if you want to play by those specific organizational standards or not. Sure, it gets tricky. Often, those biases aren't necessarily a function of a corporate culture, but one of personal bias from people in leadership roles throughout the particular organization. So, your bottom line becomes, what are the impressions you desire to send about your personal image, and how can you best direct those?

As a young professional or someone wanting to reposition your personal brand, your personal style may be an elusive beast at best. You're certainly entitled to appreciate new styles and the ever-evolving multitude of fashion and beauty trends. Still, some things don't need to change. I'm referring to more than your fashion, beauty, and grooming choices. I'm referring to how your clothes fit, your energetic vibe, the swagger in your steps, and the pride in your heart. Own it.

ORGANIZE YOUR WARDROBE AND PLAN YOUR OUTFITS

If you want your style to come across as professional, feminine, or masculine, or edgy, classic, or grunge, your wardrobe and the way you style yourself should reflect that on a fairly consistent basis. If style isn't necessarily your thing, tap into the style inspiration around you. Grab your favorite fashion magazine, search fashion bloggers, or head to Pinterest to scope out looks that inspire you. Pick the ones epitomizing looks you love, and use them as inspiration for spinoff looks. Consider a signature piece or two. Audrey Hepburn rocked her cropped pants and ballet flats for decades. Former first lady Michelle Obama hasn't met a knee-length, natural-waist, belted dress that hasn't loved her. While another stylish former first lady, Jackie O., never left home without her oversized oval sunglasses.

Seasonally commit to your signature pieces and a few staple looks. Pay attention to the repeat offenders in your closet; it's no coincidence your closet has several pieces that look eerily similar. You may be naturally drawn to certain cuts, fits, fabrics, and colors. They're your style's sweet spot, your go-to staples. Head over to your closet and check it out for yourself, and while you're there, identify a few out of the ordinary pieces. You know the ones; you're absolutely in love with them and wish you could wear them every day. Consider pieces outside of your ideal taste, but that stood out to you at first sight. Grab two to three of those core pieces and style three to four staple outfits around them. Entertain yourself by mixing them up with different shoes and accessories. Play up your best features; if you have killer legs, rock above-the-knee skirts. If you're curvy, embrace your femininity with fitted-waist flounce dresses and skirts. If you have a long neck, let turtlenecks become your best friend. (Hint: nothing pulls off a great turtleneck like an elongated neck.) Meanwhile remember, nothing will ever complement your look more powerfully than your own confidence.

Personal style is just that—personal, so learn to trust your eye and instinct to embrace a style that makes you feel like the best possible version of yourself. If a feminine-meets-classic style resonates most with you, rocking edgier pieces may leave you feeling uncomfortable. You know your style; embrace it, refine it, and enjoy visually expressing yourself. As long as your image reflects and aligns with the brand you're messaging, you'll be on point.

For some people, image isn't a big priority. Still, I challenge anyone who is brand building to understand the power of the perceptions they're directing and how those impressions affect their brand. Regardless of your personal style, taking the extra time to look and feel your personal best every day can only be beneficial in building a brand. Looking and feeling fabulous (by your own standards) builds your own conviction and contributes to you feeling great about yourself.

7

Be a Little Famous: Market Yourself

Winners focus on winning. Losers focus on winners.

—*Unknown*

Once you've incorporated the four pillars of personal branding success shared in Chapter 5 to package and position your brilliance, make it your priority to educate as many people as possible in your target about your offerings. Become comfortable sharing the lessons you've learned, accomplishments you've earned, and experiences you've gained. Promote the most profound pieces from your education, career experience, internships, and extracurricular activities. Whether you're entering the job market, further establishing yourself in the marketplace, or seeking new clients, you may find yourself competing with candidates with more career experience. However, by educating others about your offerings, you can position your strengths and capabilities by highlighting what you've learned and accomplished.

As an entrepreneur, influencer, young professional, college student, or an industry expert looking to make a career move or snag more clients, implementing these personal branding tactics will help you market yourself in today's competitive marketplace.

SIX CAREER START-UP, CAREER MOVE, AND CLIENT-GARNERING TIPS FOR PROFESSIONALS

In today's job market, prepare yourself to maximize your job or new-client search. Branding makes you more marketable, visible, and fluid as a job or new-client seeker. It allows you to strategically educate others about the rational and emotional value your brand provides.

How can candidates successfully navigate the complexities of today's market? Here are six simple and effective personal branding tips to best leverage opportunities you want:

1. Be Clear about Your Goals

Focus your efforts on the jobs, clients, and companies best suited for your strengths, ideals, and career goals. Research everything there is to know about the positions and companies you're interested in. This showcases your level of passion and commitment to your search. Identify the set of skills, experiences, and personality characteristics you possess that would bring the most value to the opportunities.

Only apply for positions and vendor opportunities that match your career goals and level of experience. Applying to multiple positions in different departments within the same organization suggests you're uncertain about your career goals.

2. Identify Your Target Market or Audience

If you're not tied to a specific city, consider exploring opportunities in other cities, regions, or even countries to advance your career. There are great international opportunities for contract and consulting work. Employees within Fortune 500 companies can offer the ability to transfer to an American office after a designated time.

Identify the largest employers and contractors in your field, and apply for the opportunities that align with your capabilities and goals. Also identify companies outside your industry that are hiring for the opportunities you're seeking. Do your research; gather as much information as possible about the firms, their business models, and leadership teams.

Build a trackable list composed of each of the positions or contracts you've applied for. Include the name of the company; the human resources and hiring or contract manager's name and contact information; and the company's website, LinkedIn profile, and Twitter account. Stay abreast of relevant insight or news affecting the company and its leadership. Provide weekly follow-ups with contacts until you're called in for an interview or receive notification that you're no longer a candidate for the opportunity.

3. Develop Impactful Marketing Materials

Highlight your academic and career accomplishments, extracurricular activities, past internships (for recent graduates), and leadership qualities that will differentiate you from the competition.

Your marketing materials should include a strong branded résumé, a completed LinkedIn profile, and your elevator pitches. Imagine the conversation you'd have in the elevator with the CEO of an organization you've dreamed of working with. Remain ready and prepared to have an engaging conversation with them about what you have to offer their organization. And unless you're applying for a position as a weather girl, don't spend those few seconds discussing the weather.

Résumés and biographies tell your story to prospective employers or clients. They're job- and client-searching tools that permit you to highlight your brand attributes, strengths, and achievements. To make your résumé stand out, include your brand promise to highlight the essence of your brand story.

Consider placing your brand value in a summary section at the top of your résumé. Include a quote from a client or from a previous performance review from a manager, volunteer coordinator, professor, or internship manager. Alternatively, consider highlighting your brand value under the experience section of your résumé, accompanied with bulleted accomplishments.

In creating your branded résumé:

- Highlight your brand promise in a summary section at the top, while reinforcing it in other parts of the résumé.

- Show your passion and enthusiasm regarding your work.
- Write an accomplishment statement illustrating meaningful contributions that differentiate you from the crowd.
- Let your personality shine through using strong descriptors from Chapter 3 that give meaning to your brand.
- Highlight those experiences that support your brand and directly correlate to the specific opportunity.

4. Maximize Your Social-Network Platforms

Your social-media platforms should serve as an extension of your biography and résumé. Completely fill out your profiles, including relevant work and volunteer history, past internships, and career interests. Join alumni groups and industry associations on LinkedIn and participate within group discussions. Several times a week, engage your social platforms by sharing articles, blog posts, industry insight, and content that is relevant in your industry. You don't have to establish a profile on every platform, but do branch out to maximize your exposure.

5. Network Offline and Online

Networking remains the most effective job- and client-search strategy. With the prevalence and popularity of online career sites, publishing, and social networking, it's easy to assume using online channels exclusively is the way to go.

Thanks to the myriad of platforms on the World Wide Web, you have a lot of influence over what people can learn about you when searching your name. The Internet provides a rich opportunity to create, market, and manage your online brand.

Wherever you are in your career, why not build a great personal website to act as your online hub for your personal brand? Websites and blogs are unparalleled tools to help you gain credibility and trust while building a reputation with your target. Consider having your website house branding tools, such as your biography, speaker profile, electronic press kit, community involvement history, social-media platforms, and your contact information. A blog offers a nice way to showcase your expertise while highlighting your creative side and interests to build emotional connectivity.

Blogs give you instant accessibility to publish your ideas and perspectives to interact with readers who are interested in consuming and possibly sharing your content. Build a weekly social-media calendar and commit to posting targeted content several times a week. Likewise, social-media platforms like LinkedIn, Twitter, Facebook, and Instagram can be beneficial in promoting your personal brand. They allow you to communicate your message in your voice and personality directly with your market.

Avoid the trap of networking exclusively online. You'll run the risk of alienating and limiting your local circle of impact. Attending in-person networking, industry organizations, speaking, and social events can connect you face-to-face with your market's influencers and industry leaders. The most effective networking strategy incorporates both online and in-person connectivity. Supporting other people is an ideal way to build depth in the relationships you forge with industry professionals, influencers, associates, and your target market or audience. Be genuine about helping and supporting your network by sharing job or client leads, networking contacts, event invitations, and support. Doing so builds your own morale and strengthens the relationships you have with the people you're connected to.

6. Identify a Mentor

Identify someone who has taken an interest in you, and ask if they're open to becoming your mentor. Outline your expectations up front, and keep it simple for them. Everyone can benefit from a mentor with whom they're comfortable sharing their career goals, plans, and challenges. Your mentor can be anyone whose opinion and business acumen you respect. Consider a former manager or client, college professor, internship manager, entrepreneur, colleague, or a family member or friend.

8

Support Your Ideals through Philanthropy and Activism: Give Back

Everybody can all be great, because anybody can serve.

—Dr. Martin Luther King, Jr.

No matter what your title or role may be, or even if you don't have one, carve out time to volunteer and contribute your efforts toward those people, causes, and organizations about which you feel the most passionate. Maslow's motivational theories and other psychological research studies informs us we're driven by a host of intangible emotional forces—our need to be recognized and empowered, to have a sense of achievement, and to work toward things with meaningful purpose in life. We yearn to make positive contributions toward causes bigger than ourselves. The world needs your service, voice, and inspiration as innately as you need to give it.

As grace would have it, the more freely you share your gifts, the stronger they'll develop. Never underestimate the impact of how your knowledge, the connections you have, or the values you represent can positively influence others. Today's social and political climate has created an emotionally charged atmosphere for Americans. This presents the opportune time for you to work toward making the positive changes you want to see in the world. You can start anywhere; even small gestures of outreach and collaboration culminate in big impacts. As you nurture you sacred seed of authenticity to make your mark and cultivate your best self, aim to spread your brilliance and observe it catch fire. Trust me, the act of extending yourself to help others is one of the most empowering, gratifying, and fulfilling human needs. Empowerment breeds more empowerment. We all want to feel that we matter and belong to a community, and there is no better way to reinforce your own ability to make a difference than by sharing your time and energy with people and causes in need of your support.

Philanthropy is nourishing for the soul and helps you in strengthening your relationship with other like-minded individuals. Whether you choose to give back to someone who individually can benefit from what you have to share, you work with a group within an organization, or you start your own project, the benefits are astronomical. If you love nature, volunteer at your local botanical garden or community garden. If you love children or pets, your options are endless. Why not donate your time to a hospital or a wildlife preservation organization? There are endless opportunities, so choose causes you're interested in and passionate about. Commit yourself to giving the cause a few free hours of your time on a continual basis, write a check, or grab a few friends and initiate a for-cause project. Do something to contribute to the welfare of someone or something other than yourself. Watch how it brings joy, satisfaction, achievement, and meaningful connections to you.

Giving back is something you must experience for yourself. Do so, and you'll feel just what I'm referring to. Something magical happens when you give freely of your gifts and talents. As you commit to volunteering and giving your time or resources to the causes you choose to support, include elements of your charitable efforts to your resume and biography.

9

Brand Sustainability: Evaluate and Retool Your Personal Brand on an Ongoing Basis

Do not go where the path may lead, go instead where there is no path and leave a trail.

—*Ralph Waldo Emerson*

We all have weaker or broken places in our lives and the better we become at mending our own wounds, the better prepared we'll be in receiving our divine gifts from the world and consequently sharing our divine gifts in the world. Your experience should be one of moving onward, upward, and in tune through the adversities and joys you'll encounter along your journey.

As long as there's breath in your body and a dream in your heart, the possibilities for your sacred of authenticity and its correlating brand will be a promising work in progress. As you embark on your "on-purpose" journey, truly explore and embrace your greatest expression and the possibilities for your fullest potential. Provided you have a career, are doing business, or are committed to serving others, make it your priority to remain focused, active, and faithful. If you incorporate the branding pillars I've shared, people won't have to guess what you're up to, or what's important to you. Keep your brand's story fresh and at top of mind awareness for those you serve. In having a service to provide, you'll always have work to do and people to help.

Surrender to your 'why', your mission, and your dreams as your most trusted source in guiding your decisions to say yes to the right opportunities and no to the wrong ones. Why? Because they give meaning to your life, and meaning is what drives your motivation. Considering you have limited amounts of time and energy to expend, invest your resources in those things leading you in the direction of realizing your own dreams. Helping and providing service to yourself and others is the overarching, most profound work you'll ever do. Prioritize your own dreams and commit the necessary time and attention necessary to realize them. Only you can do that. Consequently, personal branding is a gift that gives you both the clarity and sense of direction required to concentrate your efforts around your own goals. Delivering on your "why" grants you fulfillment, joy, and a real sense of purpose—a deep appreciation and understanding around what's "on- purpose" for your particular journey: all the fire needed to blaze your own unique trail.

Read books and magazines, watch videos, and educate yourself about topics of interest. Browse the Internet and search through trustworthy websites and blogs. Expose your mind to things outside your comfort zone, and you'll be introduced to new concepts, ideas, and inspirations. Make exploring new developments, industry trajectories, businesses, and career paths one of your guilty pleasures. They'll remind you how expansive, creative, and evolutionary humanity is. The variety of ways in which you can discover ideal scenarios for your life becomes the means to do your "on-purpose" work while making a living and realizing your dreams. There's so much more to explore, know, and enjoy; a lifetime just isn't enough! So what are you waiting for?

Never compromise yourself, your values, your worth, or your potential. Live your own truth, and trust your gut, no matter what. It's where your power lives. Have a sense of wonder and remain curious. Prioritize time to do the things that give you joy and that you care deeply about. That's where your light will shine brightest. Dream, work, achieve—and then dream bigger, achieve more, and keep building. Honor the magic of your inner power, that knowingness that patiently lingers through the distraction until it's heard. Have patience with yourself, but respect the lessons. The world and all it has to offer were created for you to explore, enjoy, and evolve. Give from your heart, create from your mind, and listen in silence to your inner voice of guidance. Trust what it says, and dare to gamble on that. Dream big, brand smart, and execute, execute, execute!

Your self-awareness, achievements, areas of interest, and ambitions will evolve as you gain more knowledge, experience, and specialties. In an effort to stay on top of your own progression, every four to six months, access your brand's story, and choose one or two personal initiatives. Make it a conscious effort to bridge the gap between who you are and who you aspire to become.

Consider closing your brand's gap between how you view your brand today versus where you'd like to see it evolve:

- Advance your education (earn an advanced degree, take a class at a local college, and enroll in an online class).
- You're expected to make mistakes; as you do, own up to them, take the lesson, and then quickly move on.
- Although what you say won't build your brand alone, it can undermine what you've worked to build, so think before you speak or post.
- Be responsive and responsible. Your personal brand is built around servicing your target; show the people you're serving you respect their time.
- Know and act when it's time to gain additional work experience, and start preparing for your next career move.
- Explore a new opportunity to volunteer or mentor someone in an area in which you have expertise, interest, or passion.
- Exhibit good behavior every time you're in public; you represent your brand, whether you're at a fundraiser or the beauty salon. Eyes are watching.
- Stay focused; becoming scattered could dilute your brand. If you attempt to take on too many tasks, you appear to lack focus, making it unclear what you stand for or are good at.

- Consider a scalable coaching or mentoring opportunity if you have a talent, skill, or leadership abilities you'd like to share.
- Your "on-purpose" brand is built around your authenticity. Ignore trends that aren't true to you; build and sustain your brand, your ideals, your truth, your aspirations, and your goals.

Experience is the most renewable attribute in building an "on-purpose" brand that can sustain your evolution. As you grow, your personal brand's story should reflect that growth. In having more life-altering experiences and connecting with more people, it's natural to reprioritize your brand's nonnegotiables. As often as you update your résumé and bio, take a look at the other elements of your brand to make sure you're still moving in the direction of your dreams. Revisit your marketing pieces, elevator pitch, image, online profiles, and networking strategy. Evaluate your short-, medium-, and long-term goals. Maintain messaging that aligns with both what you're doing now and are working toward.

Don't say 'yes' or 'no' easily when making commitments. Remain open toward new experiences, projects, trainings, and networking opportunities. Shy away from nonconducive, negative, or idle commitments. Gone are the days of folks haphazardly going through life working and building other people's dreams without working toward their own. Surely there is value in serving before you lead; but you'll always serve, so making your mark by nurturing your own sacred seed of authenticity is a by-product of dreaming big, branding smart, and blazing a trail in your life.

Notes

1. Dana R. Carney, Amy J. C. Cuddy, and Andy J. Yap. "Power Posing: Brief Nonverbal Displays Affect Neuroendocrine Levels and Risk Tolerance." *Psychological Science* (2010), accessed January 6, 2017. doi: 10.1177/0956797610383437.

2. Eric Barker. "How to Flirt-Backed by Scientific Research." *Time.* April 14, 2014, accessed January 6, 2017. http://time.com/59786/how-to-flirt-backed-by-scientific-research/.

3. Karen J. Pine. "Mind What You Wear: The Psychology of Fashion." KarenPine.com, accessed January 6, 2017, http://karenpine.com/research/fashion-psychology/.

4. Tom Rath. "StrengthsFinder 2.0." Gallup Press, 2007. Accessed January 6, 2017.
   http://strengths.gallup.com/110440/About-StrengthsFinder-20.aspx

MAKE YOUR MARK: PERSONAL BRANDING JOURNAL

Personal Branding Journal

Personal Branding Journal

Personal Branding Journal

_____

_____

_____

_____

_____

_____

_____

_____

_____

_____

_____

_____

_____

_____

_____

_____

_____

_____

_____

_____

_____

_____

Personal Branding Journal

Personal Branding Journal

_____

_____

_____

_____

_____

_____

_____

_____

_____

_____

_____

_____

_____

_____

_____

_____

_____

_____

_____

_____

_____

_____

Personal Branding Journal

Personal Branding Journal

_____

_____

_____

_____

_____

_____

_____

_____

_____

_____

_____

_____

_____

_____

_____

_____

_____

_____

_____

_____

_____

_____

Personal Branding Journal

Personal Branding Journal

_____

_____

_____

_____

_____

_____

_____

_____

_____

_____

_____

_____

_____

_____

_____

_____

_____

_____

_____

_____

_____

_____

_____

Personal Branding Journal